from Soup to Nuts

by Gloria Lesser Rothstein

SCHOLASTIC
PROFESSIONAL BOOKS

New York • Toronto • London • Sydney • Auckland

To my sons, Ryan and Hale—who taught me all about celebrating differences.

Acknowledgments
Many ... Thanks

I'd like to thank Carol Mears, pre-first grade teacher at Pine Crest School in Boca Raton, Florida, for her contributions to this project. From reviewing the units, to testing recipes, to generously sharing her insights and expertise, she added a very special flavor. Plus, a note of thanks to all the teachers who helped me gain a better understanding of cooking in the classroom.

I wish to thank Reiko Nishioka, Director of Education at the Morikami Museum in Delray Beach, Florida, for introducing me to Japanese culture and food. Also, thanks to the American Egg Board and the Tea Council of the U. S. A. for the information they provided.

A very special thanks to Terry Cooper, Editor in Chief of Scholastic Professional Books...Helen Moore Sorvillo, Associate Editor...and Judy Farer, editor...for adding all the right ingredients to this project.

I'd also like to thank my mom for her secret recipe. Wherever I go—I know she's always behind me.

To my sons, Hale and Ryan, my family, and my friends—Thanks for your support, encouragement, love...and for making such a difference in the way that I see the world.

Copyright ©1994 by Gloria Lesser Rothstein
Cover and interior design by Vincent Ceci
Cover and interior illustration by Claude Martinot

0-590-49650-6

Printed in U.S.A.
12 11 10 9 8 7 6 5 4 3 2 1

CONTENTS

INTRODUCTION

> Variety's the very spice of life,
> That gives it all its flavor.
> — *William Cowper*

Variety, spice, life, flavor! What would happen if I mixed these ingredients together? I'd create the perfect recipe for a new book. That's how *From Soup to Nuts* began. Combining some fresh ideas with a dash of spice created a teacher-friendly resource book with a multi-cultural flavor.

By bringing food and cooking into the classroom, I knew that I could give children a taste of the world. With a hands-on approach, I would blend literacy, cultural diversity, and fun.

Using subjects such as soup, bread, beans, or nuts, I wanted to explore differences — in foods, in tastes, in people, and in cultures.

Learning to appreciate and celebrate these differences was an exciting way to expand horizons and introduce children to a world of possibilities.

All Kinds of Literature

From the fiction and nonfiction read-alouds, to the fables, folktales, myths, legends, tall tales, photo essays, chants, poems, and nursery rhymes, this literature-based program includes quality books and stories to introduce children to a variety of foods and flavors.

Enjoying the Multicultural Flavor

Sample foods and dishes from other countries. Learn about the customs, traditions, and beliefs of others. Find out how different people cook, serve, and use the same foods. Discover how food brings people together—within your classroom and around the world.

Different Ways of Learning

Use the literature as a springboard for discussions, cooking, tasting, and a variety of cross-curriculum projects and activities. As you cook, integrate math, science, language, history, geography, sociology, and art. Add interactive charts, displays, collections, recipes, dramatic play areas, games, surveys, interviews, and other hands-on materials.

Learning from Others

Realize how much children can learn about food and culture from each other, from family members, and from community resources. Whether you invite people to visit the classroom, or go on field trips or outings, picture what sharing food, breaking bread, sipping tea together, or exchanging recipes can add.

Cooking, Tasting, and Recipes

Whether you try all the recipes in the book, or just a few, remember that cooking is about experimenting, being creative, making choices, and trying new things. I loved the idea of reading recipes, writing recipes, using recipes, and making recipe books. I hope you will too.

THE COOK'S TOUR

After talking to a number of teachers, I realized that every cook must experiment with what works best — even in the classroom. Whether you are using a fully equipped kitchen, or bringing in a small electrical appliance or two — being well prepared is definitely the secret to success.

Try the recipes ahead of time. That way, there are no surprises. If it's more convenient, use a commercial mix instead of a pancake, pudding, or cornbread recipe. Whichever recipe you're going to use, write it in simple terms or pictures so that it's easy for everyone to read and follow. Create one large chart or individual recipe cards.

In keeping with the theme of appreciating differences, know which of your children have dietary restrictions. Make sure you're aware of the foods that can't be eaten, and find suitable alternatives.

Take time to emphasize the importance of good health and safety habits. Show children how to wash their hands thoroughly using soap and water. Make thorough hand washing a prerequisite for cooking or handling food. You might wish to help children develop a set of cooking rules and regulations that focus on cleanliness and on the use of cooking equipment. Post these in a prominent place as an easy reminder.

Most of the time, you'll probably cook with small groups. It's easier and more enjoyable for children. Occasionally, a cooking activity can be done with the class. For any project, consider asking a parent to work with you or to help with the cleanup.

Although this book is filled with a variety of ideas, suggestions, and recipes, it's merely a place to begin. As you explore the world of food, your children, their parents or caregivers, and some community resource people can make a difference in your day-to-day learning. Encourage families to share ethnic recipes, prepare culturally authentic foods, or give class talks and demonstrations. Just think how children will see the world once they've had the pleasure of taking a cook's tour.

Soup

Soup is a nourishing food that can be simmered on the stove or whipped up in a blender. No matter how it's prepared — whether it's a hearty bean soup from Latin America, a goulash from Hungary, or a borscht from Russia — this basic food is enjoyed all over the world. Soup is chock full of connections with customs, traditions, stories — all interesting ways to get a taste of other cultures.

Chicken Soup with Rice
Maurice Sendak

Enjoy soup throughout the year with this delightful rhyme by Maurice Sendak. *Chicken Soup with Rice* is the perfect introduction to a discussion of when people eat soup, where people eat soup, how people eat soup, and what kinds of soup people eat.

The first time you read the book aloud, suggest that the children sit back, relax, and enjoy its flavor. As you reread the story, encourage children to join in when it's time for "chicken soup with rice."

After You Read

Children close their eyes and picture a big bowl of chicken soup, then describe how it looks, smells, and tastes. They might discuss the kinds of chicken soup they have eaten.

As children share experiences, bring out that people all over the world eat chicken soup on various occasions: on chilly days, warm summer days, sick days, holidays, special occasions — for lunch, for dinner, for a snack — at the beginning of a meal, as the meal — with rice, with noodles, with dumplings, with wontons, with matzoh balls. Children can build this list with you.

Using an Interactive Chart

To help children discover that there are many different ways to eat chicken soup, create a chicken soup with _____ pocket chart. Place blank cards near the chart and invite youngsters to write a word that could replace rice. Students will enjoy seeing the many variations and watching the word pile grow.

Before You Cook

In the story, a boy has visions of going to far-off Spain, old Bombay, and paddling down the Nile on a crocodile. On a map or globe, locate each of these places. Children can talk about what it might be like to travel to other countries.

Mention that although chicken soup may be eaten all over the world, the way it is prepared and served differs from country to country and from people to people. Point out that in Spain, chicken soup might be made with parsnips, turnips, tomatoes, carrots, celery, chicken, and rice.

Since adding eggs to chicken soup is not something most children expect, it's a nice way to encourage children to try something new and to sample food from China. Watch children make all kinds of interesting discoveries as they help you cook Egg Drop Soup.

As You Cook

• Talk about words that have more than one meaning. Call attention to the words *beat* and *add*.
• Predict what will happen to the broth when you add cornstarch; predict what will happen to the broth when you add the eggs. While cooking, have the children make their own observations.
• Mention that there are different ways to cook food. Point out that many Chinese dishes are prepared very quickly. Emphasize why it is important to organize all ingredients beforehand.
• Mention that some people call this Egg Flower Soup. Encourage children to imagine why.

Egg Drop Soup
(Serves 8-10)

Equipment:

soup pot, slotted spoon, fork, ladle, knife, plastic measuring cups and spoons, 3 small mixing bowls, plastic bowls and spoons.

Ingredients:

6 cups chicken broth
2 eggs
2 tablespoons cornstarch
4 tablespoons water
1 scallion finely chopped (optional)

Teacher:

• Bring 6 cups of chicken broth to a rapid boil.
• Meanwhile: Chop the scallion into fine bits and set it aside in a bowl.
• Beat the 2 eggs in a second bowl.
• In the third bowl, put the 2 tablespoons cornstarch.
• Gradually stir 4 tablespoons cold water into the cornstarch, until the mixture is free of lumps.
• When the chicken soup is boiling rapidly, give the cornstarch mixture a brief stir and gradually pour it into the soup. Keep stirring until the broth thickens. Then, slowly add the beaten eggs, stirring constantly with a slotted spoon until the eggs form threads in the soup.
• If desired, top with scallions.
• Serve.

Book-Related Activities

• **Review the names of the months.** Help children recall what makes each month memorable in *Chicken Soup with Rice*. Have the class work together to make a memorable book of their own. As an ongoing project, children can record the highlights of each month. Since you will be cooking and doing many food-related activities, this booklet or big book (whichever you prefer) would be a nice way to remember the year, month by month.

• **Discuss the four seasons.** Ask children to think about how seasonal changes affected the boy in *Chicken Soup with Rice*. Decide how seasonal changes influence people's lifestyles. Help youngsters realize that climate affects what people wear, what they do, and what they eat.

• **Recognize National Soup Month.** Although every month is soup month in *Chicken Soup with Rice*, the month of January is actually National Soup Month. Share this information with children and have them decide why they think January is a good month to promote interest in soup. As a group activity, make a list of things children could do to encourage others to eat soup.

• **Encourage children to share what they know about China.** On a map or globe, help children locate China. If possible, invite a parent to visit the classroom for a cooking demonstration, or to talk about Chinese foods, holidays, or traditions.

• **Begin food journals.** Suggest that children use these journals to describe their own reactions to cooking experiences, new foods, stories, and projects. Point out that they can use single words, pictures, and/or complete sentences.

Name_____

Tell your own story. Think of a soup for your favorite month. Draw a picture.

●

_____

MONTH

Teacher's Note: To extend the soup theme throughout the year, have children name or illustrate a different soup for each month. Set aside time for children to compare selections.

A BOOK TO READ ALOUD

Growing Vegetable Soup
Lois Ehlert

Learn how to make vegetable soup with Lois Ehlert's delightful presentation. *Growing Vegetable Soup* starts with planting the seeds, and ends with a delicious bowl of soup. The book provides a clear picture of the step-by-step process.

As you read the book aloud, help children make interesting discoveries about the text, art, and labels. Use the book to introduce key words such as *soup, pot, bowl, ladle,* and *spoon.*

After You Read

Children make a list of the vegetables used in Lois Ehlert's vegetable soup and talk about the vegetable soups they have eaten. As children make comparisons, help them realize that there are many different ways to make vegetable soup. People choose the ingredients to use in soup. Choices are different and change. Ask volunteers to name vegetables they would select.

Before You Cook

Children recall which vegetables were used in *Growing Vegetable Soup*. Discuss the fact that people use what's available when making soup. Develop the concept that different crops are grown in different parts of the world. Ask children to name vegetables grown in their area and decide which ones could be used in soup.

Since most children expect soup to be hot, prepare a soup that requires no cooking. Make Gazpacho, a cold vegetable soup from Spain.

Mention that some people make Gazpacho spicy — especially if they live in hotter climates. Spicy foods cause a person to perspire, and perspiring helps the body cool off.

Book-Related Activities

• **Write Lois Ehlert's recipe for vegetable soup.** Emphasize the importance of writing a recipe step-by-step. Help children develop a simple explanation of the steps to follow.

Mary, Mary, quite contrary,

How does your garden grow?

With _____ and _____
         (noun)   (noun)

And _____ _____ all
         (adjective)   (noun)

in a row.

• **Create your own garden of verses.** Ask each child to write a rendition of the Mother Goose Rhyme, "Mary, Mary, Quite Contrary." Youngsters can use words or pictures to complete the rhyme.

• **Play "Categories."** This leg-tapping, hand-clapping, finger-snapping circle game is an example of something passed down from generation to generation. Have children sit in a circle and chant "Categories" (follow with names of vegetables or vegetable soups).

• **Invite a Spanish-speaking guest** to visit the classroom to teach a song, a game, or read aloud an age-appropriate selection in Spanish.

• **Develop sensory awareness.** Children talk about soups that are hot, cold, thick, creamy, and so on. Encourage children to describe special soups they have eaten.

Gazpacho
(Serves 8-10)

Equipment:

a blender, cutting board, knife, plastic knives, plastic measuring cups and spoons, ladle, bowls, and spoons

Ingredients:

4 tomatoes (or a 28-oz can of whole tomatoes)
1 large green pepper
1 large cucumber
1 small onion (to yield 1/4 cup when chopped)
2 tablespoons olive oil
1 tablespoon wine vinegar
Salt and pepper
Croutons

Teacher:

• Wash all vegetables.
• Cut the tomatoes into chunks.
• Cut the green pepper and cucumber into small pieces.
• Chop the onion.
• In a blender, combine tomatoes, green peppers, cucumbers, and 1/4 cup chopped onion
• Cover and blend on medium speed until smooth.
• Add the 2 tablespoons olive oil, 1 tablespoon wine vinegar, and salt and pepper to taste.
• Blend thoroughly. Chill for one hour.
• Serve with croutons.

LISTENING/STORYTELLING: *A Fable*

All over the world, people enjoy similar foods. How these foods are cooked and served is what sparks interest. This analogy applies to many stories. For example, Aesop's fables are teaching tales that have been enjoyed all over the world for centuries. Although his fables have been told again and again, every culture has different versions. Every storyteller does, too. Share the fable, "The Fox and the Stork," with the class and see how they respond to your version.

Fox invited Stork to his home for dinner. Carefully, he set out two large, shallow dishes of delicious soup. Fox lapped up the soup with great pleasure, while Stork just stood there and struggled. No matter how hard she tried—because of her long bill—she couldn't even get one drop of soup. This made Fox laugh. So, soon after, Stork invited Fox for dinner. Stork served soup in pitchers with long, narrow necks. This time, Stork found it easy to enjoy the soup; however, poor Fox couldn't even get a taste.

• Have the children retell this story in their own words or through pictures, in class or outside of school. Help youngsters appreciate how each person adds something different to a story.
• Explain that this kind of story was used to teach valuable lessons. Ask children what they learned from this fable. Then encourage them to determine how the following sayings apply to "The Fox and the Stork":
• One good turn deserves another.

Name_____

Make vegetable soup. Pick some vegetables. Put them in the pot.

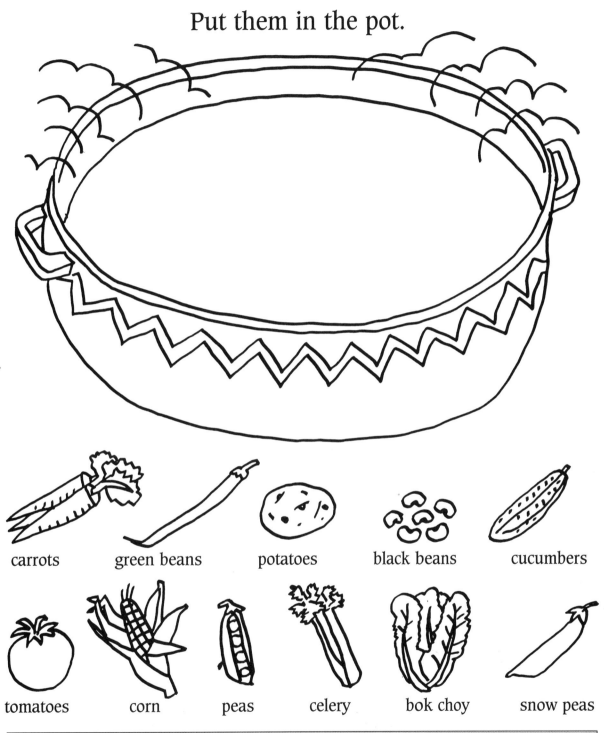

carrots   green beans   potatoes   black beans   cucumbers

tomatoes   corn   peas   celery   bok choy   snow peas

Teacher's Note: To help children discover that vegetable soup can be made with many combinations, have each child pick and add the vegetables of choice to the pot by cutting out the vegetables at the bottom of each page and pasting them in the pot.

- He who laughs last laughs best.
- Have children discuss ways to serve soup. Mention bowls, mugs, tablespoons, ladles, crocks, kettles, and tureens. Encourage children to tell how soup is served at home.
- Read another version of this fable in *Anno's Aesop* by Mitsumasa Anno, a well-known children's book author/illustrator from Japan.

APPRECIATING DIFFERENCES

Read *Stone Soup*, the Caldecott Honor book by Marcia Brown. In this old French folktale, some hungry soldiers cleverly find a way to get the people of the village to help them make soup from three round, smooth stones.

Also read *Stone Soup* by Tony Ross and/or *Stone Soup* by Ann McGovern.

Encourage the children to make comparisons between the stories. Focus on how the stories are alike and how they are different. Poll the class to see which version each child prefers. Develop the concept that people have different tastes and opinions.

More Books About Soup

Today Is Monday
by Eric Carle

A wonderful book for introducing the days of the week, enjoying soup (zoop), focusing on children all over the world, and bringing music and song into the classroom.

Alphabet Soup:
A Feast of Letters
by Scott Gustafson

A beautifully illustrated book that could be used to stir up some interest in alphabet soup, housewarming parties, and the units on bread, tea, beans, and potatoes.

Eating the Alphabet:
Fruits and Vegetables
from A to Z
by Lois Ehlert

A colorful tour of the world of fruits and vegetables, Lois Ehlert style. The glossary at the back of the book provides background information on fruits and vegetables from many lands, so it can also be used with some of the other food units.

Vegetable Soup
by Jeanne Modesitt

A delightful book about vegetable soup and the importance of tasting new foods. There's even a recipe on the last page.

An Angel for Solomon Singer
by Cynthia Rylant

A heartwarming story about a lonely old man who finds comfort and a special kind of nourishment at the Westway Cafe in New York City.

Monkey Soup
by Louis Sachar

A lighthearted look at a child's view of the perfect soup to cure her father's cold. Since the mother is busy making chicken soup, it's a natural for this unit.

Why the Sky Is Far Away:
A Folktale from Nigeria
retold by Mary-Joan Gerson

An interesting way to give children a taste of another culture and to show that learning to respect and care for the environment is far from a new idea.

Theme-Related Activities

A Soup Spot

Stir up some interest in soup by stocking a corner of the room with a soup pot, ladle, wooden spoon, plastic measuring cups, measuring spoons, plastic soup bowls, soup spoons, empty soup cans, pot holders, and aprons. Children can use the corner for pretending or for cooking demonstrations.

SOUPer Market

Children develop an appreciation of the great variety of soups that exist. Invite them to cut soup pictures from old magazines and post them on a bulletin board. Everyone can enjoy working together to label items and create a SOUPer market.

SOUPer STARS

Children construct and interpret pictographs. Invite children to choose 4 or 5 popular soups which you then list on a Souper Stars pictograph. Give each child a small circle made from colored construction paper. The child crayons a happy face on the circle and places it on the pictograph next to a favorite soup. Once the pictograph is complete, help children identify which soup is the favorite, which is least popular, and so on.

The Scoop on Soup

Everyone can gather interesting information about soup by talking to friends, neighbors, and familiar persons in the community. Encourage children to find out about customs and traditions, the way soup is served, the word for soup in another language, unusual soups from other countries, and stories about specific soups. Children might enjoy recording their survey on audiotape.

Recipe Booklets

To involve parents and caregivers in each unit, invite them to contribute favorite recipes. Children can bring in easy-to-prepare soup recipes that are served on holidays, or that are part of tradition, or that are simply favorites. Make copies for each child. Paper fasteners can be used to secure recipes between individually decorated oaktag covers. These booklets will continue to grow with each unit and can become wonderful gifts.

Name_____

For The Record
✔ the things you did. Tell about them.

❑ We talked about soup.

    I learned _____.

❑ We read books about soup.

    I read _____.

❑ We made soup.

    I liked _____.

❑ We made different things

    I liked _____.

❑ We worked together.

    We _____.

Teacher's Note: As children complete this checklist, they will remember highlights of the unit and things they'd like to share outside of school. They can also see that people do have different tastes, opinions, and interests.

Bread

All over the world, people eat bread. Most likely, it's eaten in more places and in greater quantities than any other food. French bread, Italian bread, Russian rye, pita, challah — bread comes in all shapes and sizes and can be made in many different ways. Whether it's long and thin, plump and round, soft and flat, or thin and hard, bread is important to people everywhere.

This Is the Bread I Baked for Ned
Crescent Dragonwagon

Discover the pleasures of baking bread through this cumulative tale told in verse. *This Is the Bread I Baked for Ned* colorfully illustrates a meal centered around bread and conveys the joy of sharing it.

The first time you read the book, suggest that children sit back and enjoy the sights and sounds. As you reread the book, encourage children to join in for recurring phrases.

After You Read

Talk about the picture of the braided bread baked for Ned. Ask children to recall the last time they shared food with a friend. You may wish to mention that the word *companion* comes from the Latin words *cum* (with) and *panis* (bread) and means "someone with whom you share bread." Point out that sharing food has always been a special way of showing friendship.

Share a braided bread in the classroom. If possible, bring in a challah — a braided egg bread, traditionally served by Jewish families all over the world. As part of the Sabbath meal, prayers are said over this bread, and then the family breaks bread together. Everyone present must eat a piece of bread. Point out that people everywhere have customs and traditions that center around bread.

Using an Interactive Chart

• Create a pocket chart with pictures of bread and a sentence reading "This is the bread I baked for _____." Place blank cards near the chart. Children can write a friend's name on a card and place it in the chart.

• A variation would be a pocket chart that reads: "This is the _____ I baked for Ned." A variety of bread cards with pictures on one side and words on the other would give children some hands-on experience with different kinds of bread.

Before You Cook

Talk about baking bread and the special cozy feeling that freshly baked bread gives.

Give each child a straw and a small paper cup with dishwashing liquid dissolved in warm water. Ask them to blow gently into the liquid, using their straws. Encourage children to offer their ideas about what made bubbles form. Then turn the discussion to bread-making. Invite children to discuss why they think yeast is used to make bread. To confirm their understanding, you may wish to mix some yeast in a little lukewarm water and sugar. Pour it into a bottle and put a deflated balloon over the neck. (Stretch it out a bit to ease inflation later.) Have children observe what happens. Have them look at slices of bread. Can they see the air bubbles?

Mention that Crescent Dragonwagon, author of *This Is the Bread I Baked for Ned*, actually owns an Arkansas inn with her husband, Ned. (You may wish to locate Arkansas on a map.) Crescent Dragonwagon's hobby is cooking, and she used to do some of the cooking for the inn. Most likely, the author has had the pleasure of sharing homemade bread with interesting travelers from all over the country. Discuss what can be learned by visiting different parts of the country.

Biscuits
(Makes 12)

Equipment:

mixing bowl, fork
or pastry blender,
plastic measuring cups
and spoons, cookie sheet

Ingredients:

2 cups all-purpose flour
1 tablespoon baking powder
1 teaspoon salt
1 cup milk
1/4 cup margarine
(extra margarine to grease
cookie sheet)

Teacher:

• Lightly grease the cookie sheet.
• In the mixing bowl, combine 2 cups flour, 1 tablespoon baking powder, and 1 teaspoon salt.
• Blend the 1/4 cup margarine into this mixture until it resembles fine crumbs.
• Stir in 1 cup milk, until it forms a dough.
• Knead the dough gently.
• Divide the dough into 12 equal portions, shape and place them on the cookie sheet.*
• Bake at 450° for 15 minutes, or until brown.

Keep one unbaked biscuit aside if you have decided to do the what-makes-dough-rise activity in As You Cook.

Suggest that trying homemade biscuits would be an interesting way to get a taste of the South. This quick bread — an African-American favorite that is popular all over the South — is easy to prepare and is very similar to an English scone.

As You Cook

• As you do each of these steps during cooking, encourage children to predict what they think will happen. Encourage children to describe results orally after each step.
• Explain that the word *biscuit*, like many other food words, are borrowed from other languages. Biscuit actually comes from the French words *bis*, meaning "again" and *cuire*, meaning "to cook." It means "twice-baked." The biscuits being prepared are only baked once. Some children may be interested in finding out why the French baked their biscuits twice and sharing their information with the class.
• When the biscuits have cooled, invite children to compare the unbaked biscuit to a baked one. What changes have taken place? Record their observations.
• Have children share their ideas about what they think made the biscuit dough rise. If you did the yeast activity before cooking, children will know that it has something to do with bubbles. (In the presence of moisture, the acid and the alkali in baking powder react to form a gas. This gas forms tiny bubbles in the dough. Since the bubbles expand quickly, so does the dough.)
If you did not do the yeast activity, you may wish to have children experiment adding baking powder to different liquids such as water, vinegar, or milk, and then form their hypotheses. Split a baked biscuit open, and have children look for air holes.

Book-Related Activities

• **Count your way through the book** *This Is the Bread I Baked for Ned.* To stimulate discussion, you may wish to ask such questions as: How many tulips were in the jug? How many soup bowls were set? How many unexpected guests arrived? How many pets came? How many different things were there to eat? How many people helped clean up?

• **Look at words that sound the same, but do not have the same spellings or meanings.** Talk about the words *dough/doe, knead/need,* and *flour/flower.*

• **Decide what makes this story unique.** Children describe cumulative tales they've heard. You may wish to mention that rhythmic, cumulative tales are part of many cultures and are enjoyed by children all over the world.

• **Talk about the musical instruments mentioned in the story.** Children discuss why one of the guests brought musical instruments to the gathering and what music adds to a party. They describe the various kinds of music they have enjoyed at celebrations. Ask about the instruments, music, and songs. Help children share and appreciate cultural   differences.

• **Invite primary caregivers to visit and share information about ethnic foods, customs, or traditions.** Crescent Dragonwagon is the daughter of Charlotte Zolotow, a well-known children's book author. This bit of information could lead to a lively discussion about interesting and valuable things children learn from their mothers and/or primary caregivers. To bring out the fact that Crescent Dragonwagon's experience is true of children everywhere, you may wish to invite mothers and primary caregivers to visit and share some simple information about their cultural foods, customs, or traditions.

• **Explore ways to welcome.** The Russian word for hospitality means "bread and salt." Serving a freshly baked loaf of bread along with a bowl of salt is an old Russian custom — an expression of respect, honor, and friendship. Children discuss what they do to make others feel welcome. They can also share some of their own experiences of being welcomed.

Name_____

Plan a special menu. Start with bread.

The bread baked for Ned	The bread I would bake
The food made for Ned	**The food I would make**
Some friends who came 1. _____ 2. _____ 3. _____ 4. _____	**Four friends who would come** 1. _____ 2. _____ 3. _____ 4. _____
How they had fun _____ _____ _____	**What I would do for fun** _____ _____ _____

Teacher's Note: This menu planning activity can be completed with words and/or pictures. As children recall the colorful meal made for Ned, they will get ideas for their own meal planning.

A BOOK TO READ ALOUD

Bread, Bread, Bread
Ann Morris

Take a trip to other lands with Ann Morris's colorful photographs and lively text. *Bread, Bread Bread* is easy to read and a perfect introduction to the world of bread. The photo index at the back of the book provides background information on a variety of breads and cultures as well as interesting information about each picture.

Invite children to travel through the book with you and learn about bread in other lands. The first time you read the book aloud, encourage the children to observe how the text travels through the pages.

After You Read

Talk about the variety of breads depicted in Ann Morris's book. Find out how many children have tasted each of the breads shown. Ask children to name other breads they've tasted. Call attention to the photos of the Indian family and the flat bread they are eating. Point out that in India, it is customary to eat with your fingers.

Before You Cook

Help children locate India on a map. Explain that the most popular bread eaten in India is called *chapati* (ch pat' e or che pa' te). This bread is flat because it's made without leavening agents. Remind children of the difference between leavened and unleavened bread. Mention that chapati is prepared quickly on a hot griddle and is served in India, in some parts of Africa, and in the Caribbean. The Caribbean version of this bread is called *roti* and is sold by street vendors. It can be wrapped around a variety of fillings and eaten on the go.

Book-Related Activities

• **Gather information about other flat breads eaten around the world.** Mention *injera*, a flat, chewy bread eaten in Ethiopia. Point out that it's made from a special grain which grows in that country. See how many other flat breads children can name.

• **Make a Bread, Bread, Bread book.** Children fill it with writings and pictures about bread from other lands. Children can recall information learned from the story and find their own creative ways to share this material with others. Assemble the book and display it in the classroom.

• **Add to the food journals.** Children jot down reactions to stories, activities, and bread-making.

LISTENING/STORYTELLING: *A Folktale*

Like recipes, folktales are handed down from generation to generation. True to tradition, they change and develop. Folktales provide important commentaries on relationships and behavior. They teach basic lessons about getting along in society.

Before you share this version of "The Little Red Hen," mention that the tale originated in England. Since most children will be familiar with the story, invite audience participation. Suggest that children supply the voices of cat, dog, and pig.

Chapati
(Makes 15-20)

Equipment:

mixing bowl with lid, spoon, plastic measuring cups and spoons, rolling pin(s), electric frying pan, spatula, platter, knife, napkins

Ingredients:

1 1/2 cups whole wheat flour
1/2 teaspoon salt
2/3 cup warm water
Oil for cooking
Stick of margarine (to serve)

Teacher:

• In a large mixing bowl, combine flour and salt. Slowly stir in water and mix until dough forms a ball. On a floured surface, knead the dough until it is smooth and sticky (5-10 minutes).
• Place it in covered bowl for 30 minutes and let it rest.
• Divide the dough into 15-20 pieces. With a rolling pin, roll each one into a circle. Lightly rub the frying pan with oil and heat it until it smokes.
• Cook the dough until it is brown and puffy on both sides.
• Serve warm with a bit of margarine.

Once there was a little red hen who found some wheat. " Who will help me plant this wheat?" she asked.

"Not I," said the cat.
"Not I," said the dog.
"Not I," said the pig.
"Then I will plant it myself," announced the hen.

After the wheat grew, the little red hen needed to harvest it and take it to the mill.
"Who will help me?" she asked.
"Not I," said the cat.
"Not I," said the dog.
"Not I," said the pig.
"Then I'll do it myself," sputtered the hen.

When the wheat was ground into flour, the little red hen decided to bake some bread.
"Who will help me make the bread?" she asked.
"Not I," said the cat.
"Not I," said the dog.
"Not I," said the pig.
"Then I'll do it myself," yelled the hen.

As a group activity, write your own Little Red Hen book. Decide who will help ✔ with the writing, ✔ with the illustrations, ✔ with proofreading and assembling the book. Make sure you add the book to your classroom library.

The bread smelled delicious as it was baking. "Now, who is going to help me eat this bread?" asked the little red hen.
"I will," said the cat.
"I will," said the dog.
"I will," said the pig.
But the little red hen shook her head and said, "No, thank you. I'd rather eat it by myself."

Name_____

Bread is important to people everywhere. How important is it to you? Find out. See how much bread you really eat. Keep a record for a week.

CALENDAR FOR A WEEK

	SUN	MON	TUES	WED	THURS	FRI	SAT
breakfast							
snack							
lunch							
snack							
dinner							
snack							

Is bread important to you? _____

Do you always eat the same kind of bread? _____

Teacher's Note: This record-keeping activity will help children make their own discoveries about the importance of bread.

APPRECIATING DIFFERENCES

• Read aloud *Hansel and Gretel*, retold and illustrated by James Marshall. In this classic German folktale, the poor woodcutter's children are abandoned in the woods with only a bit of bread.

• Also read aloud *Hansel and Gretel*, the Caldecott Honor book by Rika Lesser, to provide an award-winning version of the same tale.

• Encourage children to tell how these versions are the same and how they are different. Find out which version is the class favorite. Take a vote.

• Have the children recall how Hansel turned bread into bread crumbs. Ask children to think of other ways to turn bread into bread crumbs. (You might even bring in a blender and bread in order to make bread crumbs.)

• Talk about how bread crumbs were used in this story. Ask children to think of additional uses for bread crumbs.

A Toast To The Author

As a child, James Marshall hated toast. Rather than eating it, he used to hide it in his bedroom closet. His closet was actually stacked with toast.

More Books About Bread

Half a Moon and One Whole Star
Crescent Dragonwagon

This bedtime treasure describes all that occurs while a young African-American girl sleeps. Winner of the Coretta Scott King award, this book has wonderful images of bread and bread-baking. You might mention that the author wrote this book while traveling in India.

From Grain to Bread
Ali Migutsch

This start-to-finish book highlights the step-by-step process of planting wheat seeds, harvesting the crop, grinding the wheat, and baking the bread. Migutsch is one of Germany's popular children's book illustrators.

Tony's Bread: An Italian Folktale
Tomie dePaola

This charming Italian folktale tells how *panettone*, the well-known Christmas bread, was originally created. The author's introduction and notes about the Italian words and expressions used in the story are helpful.

The Happy Baker
C. A. Nobens

A lighthearted story—about a baker who travels the world and is disappointed by the bread served in each country—gives readers a taste of France, Russia, Israel, India, and Mexico.

The Baker's Dozen: A Colonial American Tale
Retold by Heather Forest

In this tale, a baker learns the importance of giving and the difference between a dozen and a baker's dozen.

The Sleeping Bread
Stefan Czernecki

A Guatemalan folktale about a baker who has to figure out why, all of a sudden, his bread dough isn't rising.

Ming Lo Moves the Mountain
Arnold Lobel

Ming Lo and his wife must figure out how to move a mountain. Discovering what they do with pots and pans and loaves of bread makes this a delightful tie-in book for the unit.

Theme-Related Activities

• **Turn a bulletin board into a BREADBOARD.** Find and display pictures of breads from all over the world. Label the pictures. See how many different kinds of bread you can discover.

• **Plan a tasting party. Sample breads from different parts of the world.** Try to include breads that are unfamiliar to most children. Encourage children to share their reactions to the different tastes, and to name the winner.

• **Make BREAD BOXES.** Ask each child to bring in an empty box and transform it into a bread box. Using colored paper, glue, scissors, crayons and markers, have children cover and decorate the boxes. Anything that is bread-related can go into the box. It should be interesting to see what each child collects. At the end of the unit, the box can be taken home and shared with family members.

• **Do some practical math.** Display a packaged sliced bread. Invite students to "guestimate" how many slices are in the loaf. At snack time, have the class count the number of slices to determine whose guess came closest. Ask the children to figure out how to share the bread so that everyone present gets an equal amount. Then, invite them to share the bread.

• **Get physical.** While sitting around a classroom table, teach children this modern nursery rhyme that encourages them to move about in their chairs.

• **Collect recipes for bread.** Have children bring in recipes for holiday breads, ethnic specialties, or simply favorites. Make copies, so that the children can add them to the bread section of their recipe booklets.

An Eating Rhyme

Shake your head;
Now eat some bread.

Stretch your legs;
Now taste your eggs.

Bend your knees;
Now finish your peas.

Wiggle your feet;
Now have some meat.

First say please,
If you want cheese.

Name_____

This kind of dough is just for fun, not for eating. You can make enough for one.

You need:

flour  | salt  | water  | mixing bowl

wooden spoon | measuring spoons and cups

What you do:

Measure 1/2 cup 
3 tablespoons

Mix

Measure 1/4 cup

Add

Stir

Make

How many breads do you know? Show several in the box.

Teacher's Note: In this activity, children can follow a recipe step-by-step and experiment with kneading and shaping dough.

Tea

Tea is one of the most popular beverages in the world. People drink tea for comfort, warmth, cheer, or simply to relax. It's a drink associated with hospitality and friendship. Offering someone a cup of tea is a welcoming gesture in many cultures. From afternoon teas, to tea parties, to tea ceremonies, tea is about people.

A BOOK TO READ ALOUD

Sheep Out to Eat
Nancy Shaw

A teashop may not be ideal for all kinds of travelers. Told in rhyme, this humorous story shows how out-of-place a group of sheep are in a quaint little teashop. In a lighthearted way, *Sheep Out to Eat* takes a closer look at manners and at the formalities of teas and teashops.

As you read the book aloud, help children appreciate the bull-in-the-china-shop-type humor. The second time you read the book, encourage children to add some rhyming words.

After You Read

Talk about what it's like to go to the teashop. Have children decide what a person should and shouldn't do. Notice the things that make this little teashop fancy. Develop the concept that the setting is what makes drinking tea formal.

Using an Interactive Chart

• In this well-known nursery rhyme, "Polly, put(s) the kettle on ... and Sukey, take(s) it off again." After you teach children this original version, encourage them to rewrite the rhyme by using their own names and those of classmates. The activity can be used to bring out the importance of working together.

> _____ put the kettle on.
> _____ put the kettle on.
> _____ put the kettle on.
> We'll all have tea.
>
> _____ take it off again.
> _____ take it off again.
> _____ take it off again.
> They've all gone away.

Book-Related Activities

• **Act out the story of *Sheep Out to Eat*.** Children will enjoy using a few simple props as they demonstrate what not to do in a teashop.

• **Sing "I'm a Little Teapot."** Teach the movements and the words to this old favorite.

• **Learn about different ways to serve tea.** You may wish to mention that afternoon tea is enjoyed by people in England, in India, in Argentina, and in many other parts of the world. Encourage children to share what they know about when and how tea can be served. Talk about teapots, teakettles, teacups, tea sets, and so on.

• **Invite a knowledgeable guest** — parent if possible — to describe Japanese tea ceremonies and customs, or to explain how important tea is to the Chinese lifestyle.

• **Develop a recipe for making hot tea.** Encourage children to describe, step-by-step, how to make hot tea. Record the step-by-step process on chart paper, or by posting children's illustrations; or, confirm the children's directions through an actual demonstration. If the time is right, you may wish to mention that January is National Hot Tea Month.

Sun Tea
(Serves 8)

Equipment:

2-qt clear glass jar with lid,
plastic measuring cup, teapot, cups,
spoons, a serving platter, a doily, napkins

Ingredients:

6 herbal tea bags
6 cups plain water
Plain tea biscuits or cookies
Ice cubes

Teacher:

• Place 6 herbal teabags in a 2-quart clear glass jar.
• Measure and add 6 cups water.
• Cover. Place outdoors in full sun, or next to a window.

• Let stand for 1 to 2 hours, until it reaches desired strength.
• Remove and squeeze teabags.
• Add ice cubes and serve.

Note: Plan to look at the tea after 15 minutes, after half an hour, after an hour, and so on. Encourage the children to observe and record the changes that take place.

Enjoy your own afternoon tea. Since tea is customarily served at four o'clock, set a classroom clock to that hour. Pour the herbal tea into a teapot. Add ice. Place a doily on the serving platter before you arrange the tea biscuits. Make the setting as formal as possible. Then, invite everyone to get together for tea and biscuits.

Name_____

We Made Tea

What we used

What we did

What I saw

Teacher's Note: This activity will allow children to make their own observations and to draw their own conclusions.

May I Bring a Friend?
Beatrice Schenk de Regniers

Sometimes an invitation to tea could be for a child. *May I Bring a Friend?* is a welcoming addition to a discussion of afternoon teas and the custom of drinking tea as a gesture of friendship.

The first time you read the book aloud, bring out what an honor it would be to have tea with the King and Queen. As you reread the book, encourage children to join in with some of the dialogue.

After You Read

Encourage children to talk about the different kinds of invitations mentioned in *May I Bring a Friend?* Ask them to think about other occasions when invitations could be sent. You may wish to mention that written invitations are sent for parties and formal teas if this hasn't been discussed. Ask children to write and/or design an invitation to go along with the story. Before writing, the children decide what kind of information should be included in any invitation.

Before You Cook

Help the children plan a formal tea. Explain that at many formal teas, little tea sandwiches or finger sandwiches are served. Invite parents and primary caregivers. Have the children write the invitations. This is a valuable opportunity for families/primary caregivers to get to know each other and, possibly, to add to the children's growing knowledge about tea.

Ask the children to help you develop a list of what is needed for the tea. Have them discuss how elaborate the event should be.

Book-Related Activities

• **Learn about different ways to drink tea.** Talk about adding sugar, honey, milk, mint, and so on. Children contribute their knowledge and experience to this activity.

LISTENING/STORYTELLING: *A Legend*

Legends are another type of story passed from one generation to another. Although they cannot actually be verified, the historical explanation is usually popularly accepted.

According to Chinese legend, this is how tea was discovered around 2737 B.C.

Long ago, a Chinese emperor named Shen Nung was boiling water over an open fire. Nung always boiled water before drinking it. Although no one knew what caused illnesses, Shen Nung noticed that people who drank boiled water definitely had better health. So, this wise emperor always drank boiled water, and everyone thought of him as the "Divine Healer."

Since the servants needed branches to make the fire, the fire was made very close to the tree they used. As the water started to boil, some of the leaves from that tree blew right into the pot.

"What a marvelous smell," declared the emperor, as the aroma filled the air. And, when he took a sip, he had another pleasant surprise. The flavor was even better. And so, according to Chinese legend, tea was discovered.

• Have children work together to make a picture book to tell the story of the discovery of tea.

Bocaditos *(Makes 48)*
Tea Sandwiches from Argentina

Equipment:

knife, cutting board(s), butter spreaders, vegetable peeler, serving platter, doilies, paper towels, paper plates, teapot, teacups, teaspoons, napkins

Ingredients:

12 thin slices French bread
32 oz whipped cream cheese
1 large cucumber, thinly sliced
8 cherry tomatoes, thinly sliced
Pitted green olives, thinly sliced
Green pepper, thinly sliced

Teacher:

• Wash and dry the vegetables.
• Peel the cucumber.
• Cut vegetables into thin slices.
• Trim the crust from the bread.
• Cut each slice of bread into quarters and spread a thin layer of cream cheese on each piece.
• Top with one or two vegetable slices.
• Place doilies on the platter. Arrange finger sandwiches on the doily.
• Serve with herbal tea.

As You Cook

• Talk about fractions. As you cut bread slices in quarters, you might describe the process, cutting the slice in half, then cutting each piece into half again. (The bread is now cut into quarters.)
• Have children discuss how color and shape help to make food appealing. They can identify the colors and shapes of the ingredients for Bocaditos.
• Encourage children to be creative and experiment with different vegetable combinations, so they become aware that cooking is an art.

APPRECIATING DIFFERENCES

• Read aloud *The Town Mouse and The Country Mouse,* retold and illustrated by Lorinda Bryan Cauley. Make sure children notice that the story begins and ends with a cup of tea.
• Read aloud "City Mouse — Country Mouse" in the book *City Mouse — Country Mouse and Two More Tales* by Aesop.
• Compare Town Mouse and Country Mouse. Decide how they are alike and how they are different.
• Compare the two versions of this tale. Decide how they are alike and how they are different.

More Books About Tea

Clancy's Coat
Even Bunting

A heartwarming story that shows how an old coat and several cups of tea help to mend a broken friendship.

Thundercake
Patricia Polacco

A Russian grandmother has the perfect recipe for not being afraid of thunder. Making a thundercake and sipping tea from a Russian samovar (an urn) add a very special touch to this story — along with the recipe at the back of the book.

The King's Tea
Trinka Hakes Noble

The King's tea has to be perfect — but it's not. The milk for the tea is sour, and no one is willing to take the blame.

Name_____

People can wear fancy clothes to tea. What would you wear? Turn this t-shirt into a tea shirt.

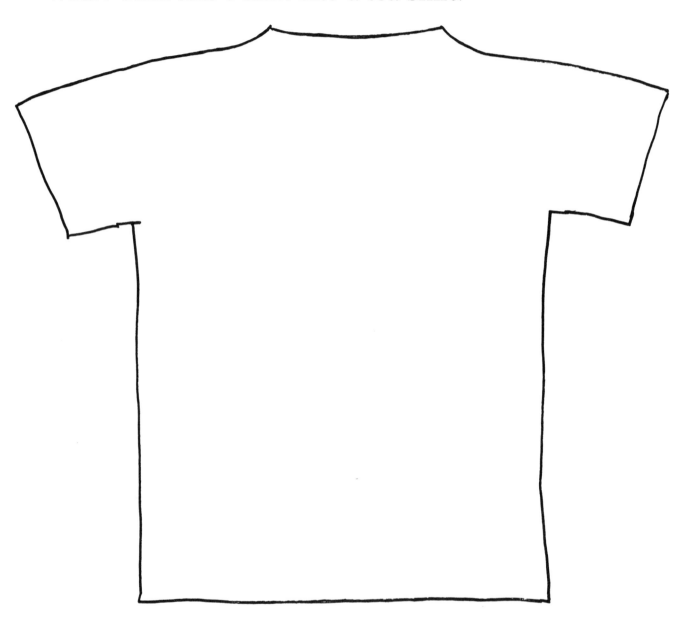

What would you have with tea?

I would have tea and_____.

Teacher's Note: Children can add sleeves, collars, ruffles, bow ties, bows, and so on — anything that turns the outline into a dressy shirt or fancy blouse.

Five Minutes' Peace

Jill Murphy

A delightful story about a Mother elephant determined to get five minutes' peace in the bathtub with a soothing cup of tea.

The Doorbell Rang

Pat Hutchins

This English author begins her story, "I made some cookies for tea." Then the fun begins.

A Birthday Basket for Tía

Pat Mora

In this story, a young Mexican girl puts together a birthday basket for her aunt. One of her special gifts is a teacup.

Tea for Two...or More: The Tea Party Book

Lucille Recht Penner

An appealing book filled with ideas, suggestions, and recipes for tea parties.

Theme-Related Activities

• **Create a Tea Room.** Turn a corner of the classroom into a little tea room. Fill the area with a teakettle, a teapot, plastic teacups and saucers, teaspoons, a serving tray, and some fancy accessories (white cotton gloves, bow ties, plastic jewelry, and so on) for dress-up. Youngsters should enjoy visiting the corner for tea parties and afternoon tea.

• **Make TEA bags.** Using crayons, markers, scissors, glue, and old magazines, children can turn small, brown lunch bags into TEA bags. As an ongoing activity, encourage youngsters to collect interesting words, pictures, and information about tea. Everyone should enjoy sharing the contents of their bags with classmates, inside and outside of school.

• **Find out where tea comes from.** On a map or globe, help children locate India, Sri Lanka, Indonesia, Kenya, and Tanzania (the major tea-producing countries). Then mention that tea is also grown in Argentina, Brazil, China, Formosa, Japan, Mozambique, Malawi, and Rwanda. Explain that tea is grown on gardens and estates in tropical or subtropical climates.

• **Paint a picture of a tea garden.** Describe workers in a tea garden plucking tea leaves off a plant. Mention that the dark green bushes are waist-high and the workers are wearing colorful clothes. They have baskets tied to their backs or balanced on their heads." Plucking," as it is called, is done by hand. The workers, using their thumbs and forefingers, pluck the upper leaves with amazing speed and toss them into their baskets. Suggest that children "act out this scene."

• **Make your own TEA Garden.** Fill a bulletin board with tea leaves. Using colored paper, design a tea bush that is covered with leaves. On each leaf, write simple directions for a tea-related activity. Youngsters should enjoy visiting the Tea Garden to pick a tea leaf.

• **Set up a TEA table**. Turn a small corner table into a TEA table. Ask children to help you fill it with different kinds of tea. Suggest that they include empty tea containers, boxes, package labels, and other items of interest. Call attention to the packages that include stories about tea and read them aloud. Use the display to show teas from around the world.

• **Collect recipes.** Ask children to bring in favorite recipes for tea cakes, tea biscuits, tea sandwiches, and so on. As part of an ongoing project, make copies so that youngsters can add them to the "tea and _____" section of recipe booklets.

Name_____

Learn more about tea. Ask someone you know.

When do you drink tea?_____

What kind of tea do you drink? _____

What kind of teacup do you use? _____

What do you add to your tea?_____

When do you serve tea?_____

Is tea part of any family tradition?_____

Share what you learn with the class._____

_____

_____

_____

_____

Teacher's Note: Suggest that children interview a parent, grandparent, or someone close to them to complete this activity. Plan time for youngsters to share their findings.

Rice

Rice is a staple food for more than half the world's population. It's a healthy, versatile grain that is the "staff of life" for many people. History, geography, agriculture, folklore and tradition — all influence the preparation and eating of rice. Anyone who looks at rice in those settings can, in a sense, get a taste of the world.

Everybody Cooks Rice
Norah Dooley

*T*ravel from house to house in Carrie's neighborhood and discover that every family cooks rice. On a street where each family comes from another land, it's easy to see that every culture has its own way of cooking and serving rice.

As you read the story aloud, develop the concept that many different families make a neighborhood. Go through the book a second time to talk about interesting details in the family pictures.

After You Read

As a group, look at the recipes in the back of the book. Help children discover that in each recipe, rice is combined with different spices and ingredients. Talk about any listed items that may be unfamiliar. If possible, pass around some spice samples and describe how they look and smell.

Talk about how specific ingredients change the taste and appearance of foods. Recall how turmeric turned the rice yellow. Decide how raisins would make rice taste. Help children realize that each culture uses different ingredients and methods of cooking.

Using an Interactive Chart

To further develop the concept that everyone cooks rice, have children think of other words and/or names that could replace Everybody. See how many possibilities youngsters can name.

Before You Cook

Mention that some families cook special rice dishes for holidays. Share an interesting Norwegian custom associated with rice pudding — a popular dessert at Christmas dinners.

Explain that the cook places one almond in this rice dish. At the holiday meal, the guest that finds the nut receives a small gift. People believe that the person who finds the nut can also look forward to a year of happiness and good luck.

Make rice pudding and, for good luck, place one almond in the bottom of each dish before serving.

As You Cook

• Give everyone a chance to smell the vanilla.
• What will cause the pudding to thicken? Ask children to share their ideas.
• Point out that using cooked rice in a recipe is a good way to use leftovers. Think of different kinds of dishes made with leftover rice.

Book-Related Activities

• **On a map or globe, locate the homelands of the families in this story.** Find Barbados, Puerto Rico, Vietnam, India, China, and Haiti. Encourage children to notice which places are large, small, close to one another, which places are islands, and so on.

• **Create an "Everybody Cooks Rice" book.** Ask each child to contribute a picture of his/her family eating a favorite rice dish. Some students might also want to write a sentence or two. Assemble the book and display it in the classroom.

Rice Pudding
(For 10)

Equipment:
plastic measuring cups and spoons, large bowl, large spoon, small bowl, fork, non-stick baking dish, 3-oz cups, spoons

Ingredients:
2 cups cooked rice*
1 cup milk
1 beaten egg
1/2 cup sugar,
1 teaspoon vanilla
Shelled almonds—one for each portion

Teacher:
• Measure the ingredients.
• In the small bowl, beat the egg.
• In the large bowl, mix 2 cups cooked rice, 1 cup milk, the beaten egg, 1/2 cup sugar and 1 teaspoon vanilla.
• Pour into the baking dish.
• Bake at 350° for 30-35 minutes until pudding thickens.

(*Note: 1 Rice Boil-a-Bag makes 2 cups of rice.)

• **Make some interesting discoveries about rice.** Bring in samples of different varieties. If possible, include long grain rice, short grain rice, brown rice, wild rice, and Basmati rice. Place the samples in sealable plastic bags, so that they can be passed around and examined.

• **Learn about potluck.** Mention that the author got the idea for this book after hosting a potluck supper in her own neighborhood. Have children predict what would happen if the people in this story had a block party or potluck dinner. Talk about how interesting the food selections would be.

• **Talk about eating rice.** Encourage children to tell about rice dishes they have eaten. Point out that in some cultures, rice is such an important part of the diet that it is eaten at every meal.

• **Plan a cooking demonstration.** To further develop the theme of this story, invite a guest to show children how to make an ethnic or holiday rice dish.

Name_____

Tell about a special picnic.

Who brings each dish? Is rice a part of your picnic?

Draw your rice picnic.

Teacher's Note: As children put the finishing touches on the community picnic, they will recall the rice dishes served in each home. Children can use their pictures to share the story at home.

A BOOK TO READ ALOUD

How My Parents Learned to Eat
Ina R. Friedman

See how important cultural differences can be in this story about the courtship of a young Japanese girl and an American sailor. The story presents an interesting view of Japanese foods, customs, and lifestyle as the couple learns about each other's ways.

Read the book aloud and help children understand that this is the story of how someone's parents fell in love. Go through the pictures in the book and have children look for contrasts in foods, customs, and lifestyle.

After You Read

Discuss the first visit to the Japanese restaurant and the American restaurant. Have children discuss how it would feel to be in unfamiliar surroundings.

Talk about the table settings in both restaurants. Encourage students to name obvious differences. Call attention to the small rice bowls. Discuss the fact that rice is served individually and that this practice shows the importance of rice in the Japanese diet.

Before You Cook

Mention that many Japanese folktales tell of rice balls or rolling rice dumplings. Rice balls are ideal food for traveling or packing in a lunch. In fact, long ago, Japanese men often carried rice balls inside a special pocket in their sleeves.

Because Japanese rice is sweet and sticky, rice balls are easy to make. Some people put a pickle (serves as a preservative) inside the ball. Others wrap the rice ball in Nori (a seaweed) or a flat, browned egg. Each cook has a personal way of preparing rice balls.

Japanese short grain rice such as Kokuhu rice can be bought at an Oriental market.

Book-Related Activities

• **Look at Japan.** Mention that Allen Say, the illustrator, was born in Yokohama, Japan. Locate Yokohama on a map. Help children recall that this is where the story takes place. Decide why this information would be of interest.

• **Learn a new way to eat.** The story points out that both the English and Americans eat with knives and forks. However, they don't eat the same way. If possible, provide sets of plastic forks and knives, so that children can try to learn to eat just as Aiko did.

• **Make a bird's nest.** Write simple directions for making a bird's nest out of mashed potatoes. Explain how to put the peas inside. Then, find out if these instructions are well written. Suggest that children try to follow them step-by-step.

• **Compare table settings.** Point out each culture in the story has its own proper way to set a table. Identify the dinner plate and bread and butter plate in the American restaurant. Talk about the rice bowl, soup bowl, teacup, and rectangular dish in the Japanese restaurant.

• **Visit a local Japanese restaurant.** Plan a class trip to give children an opportunity to learn new ways of eating and to sample new foods.

Oni Giri *(O-ne-GE-re)*
(Makes 15-20 Rice Balls)

Equipment:

plastic measuring cups and spoons, electric rice cooker (or large pot with lid), wooden spoon, ice cream scoop, individual muffin cups, a timer, a basin for water

Ingredients:

3 cups Japanese rice (Kokuhu)
4 cups water

Teacher:

• Measure the ingredients.   Put 4 cups water and 3 cups rice in pot and stir.
• Bring to a high boil and stir.
• Then, cover pot and reduce heat to lowest setting. Set the timer for 20 minutes and cook. Do not stir or remove lid.
• Allow rice to cool.
• Scoop 15 -20 individual portions of rice into muffin cups. Hand one to each child.
• Explain that a rice ball can be made the same as a snowball. Ask children to wet their hands before they begin, to keep the rice from sticking.
• Making these rice balls gives children an opportunity to taste plain rice and to eat rice in a different form.

LISTENING: *Storytelling*

While I was developing this program, I spent a great deal of time gathering materials and information. Even before I selected *How My Parents Learned to Eat*, someone shared this story with me. I thought it would be something you'd like to share with children.

A young Japanese woman was preparing to come to the United States. While attending a university here, she would be living with one of the college professors, his wife, and children. What worried her most was knowing how to eat with the family. An actual course was given at a formal restaurant in one of the big hotels. There, she would be taught how to do everything properly...including, peeling and eating a banana with a knife and fork.
The first meal she shared with the American family was a chicken dinner. Imagine how surprised she was to see everyone pick up a piece of chicken and eat it with their hands.

• Compare this to the story *How My Parents Learned to Eat*. Help children appreciate the similarities.

APPRECIATING DIFFERENCES

• Read *Bamboo Hats and a Rice Cake* by Ann Tompert. In this Japanese folktale, a couple must sell their prized possessions in order to buy rice cakes for the New Year. Key words written in Japanese are of special interest in this book, and are an important part of the text.

• Read this book a second time to appreciate how unique it is.

• Talk about the differences between our alphabet and the Japanese alphabet.

• Try to write one or two words in Japanese. Use the book as a guide.

Name_____

You learned how others eat. Let others learn about you.

Some people use a knife and fork.

Some use chopsticks.

Some use their hands.

What do you use?_____

Some sit on chairs at a table.

Some use a very low table.

Some use a cloth spread on a floor.

Where do you eat? _____

Some people eat soup with a spoon.

Some drink soup.

What do you do?_____

Teacher's Note: As children read and answer the questions, they may discover more customs they have in common with other people.

More Books About Rice

Screen of Frogs
Retold and illustrated by Sheila Hamanaka

In this old tale from Japan, a wealthy man finally discovers the importance of respecting nature. This book offers a good glimpse at rice fields and the people working in them.

The Funny Little Woman
retold by Arlene Mosel

This award-winning version of an old folktale is set in Old Japan and tells of a little old woman and her rice dumplings.

Cleversticks
Bernard Ashley

Although Ling Sung can't do what his classmates can, he finally discovers something he's good at — using chopsticks. This is another enjoyable story about learning from others.

The Boy of the Three-Year Nap
Diannne Snyder

Get a better picture of rice sacks and the Japanese way of life through this Caldecott Honor book.

In the Eyes of the Cat :
Japanese Poetry for All Seasons
Selected and Illustrated by Demi

A collection of Japanese nature poems and wonderful art.

Arroz Con Leche: Popular Songs and Rhymes from Latin America
Selected and illustrated by Lulu Delacre

Learn the words to "Rice and Milk" in English and in Spanish.

The Rice Bowl Pet
Patricia Miles Martin

A cute story about a young Chinese boy who can get a pet if he finds one small enough to fit inside a rice bowl.

Theme-Related Activities

• **Set up a Neighborhood Restaurant.** Cover a small classroom table with a tablecloth. Provide a variety of plastics — dishes, bowls, cups, knives, forks, and spoons. As children visit the corner, they can decide what kind of rice dish to serve and set the table accordingly. Then, they can actually sit down and pretend to eat a meal.

• **Make Rice Sacks.** Children turn small brown lunch bags into rice sacks by decorating them with markers, crayons, and/or magazine pictures. As an ongoing activity, children can store their rice-related papers and projects in this sack.

• **Find out where rice grows.** On a map, locate some of the countries you've talked about in this unit — Vietnam, China, India, Thailand, and Japan. Mention that rice is grown in every one of these countries. Point out that this helps to explain why rice is such an important food in Asian cultures. Ask the school librarian to help you gather information on other rice-producing countries. If possible, find and display picture of rice paddies which show people of all ages (including children) working in the fields. Talk about the fact that in some parts of the world, even young children must work.

• **Plan your own Rice Festival.** To celebrate the end of this unit, ask parents and caregivers to send in a variety of ethnic rice dishes. Also, request paper plates, plastic forks and spoons, serving utensils, and a few helpers. Display the food so that youngsters actually see how different dishes look, smell, and taste.

• **Celebrate National Rice Month** (September). The "Everybody Cooks Rice" theme could be used on a hall bulletin board or posters hung throughout the school. Use magazines, coupon fliers, and old travel folders and brochures to gather pictures of rice, rice dishes, recipes, and people eating rice. Students can work together to make collages showing that rice is important to many different people.

• **Learn about Rice Paper.** If possible, ask the art teacher to teach children about rice paper. Have her explain how it is made, how it is used, and provide some samples.

• **Make some Rice Papers.** Have children gather information about rice. Encourage them to learn about interesting customs and beliefs, about different products made with rice, and how to say the word in other languages. Suggest that every child interview someone about an aspect of rice and produce at least one rice paper.

• **Collect rice recipes.** Children bring in ethnic recipes and/or particular favorites. Make copies for children to add to the rice section of their cookbooks.

Name_____

Learn how to use these chopsticks.

What you need: a pair of chopsticks, small bowl, piece of a rice cake.

Try this.

1. Hold chopsticks straight up and down.

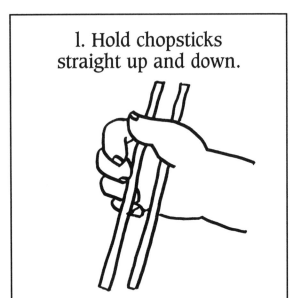

2. Move the two chopsticks apart.

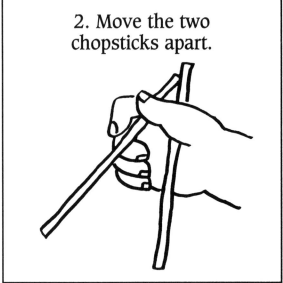

3. Manipulate food with chopsticks.

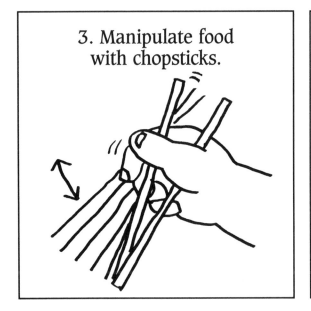

4. Hold a piece of rice cake.

Teacher's Note: Through this activity, children can gain practice in following directions and can learn to eat in a new way. (Packages of chopsticks are available at the supermarket.)

Potatoes

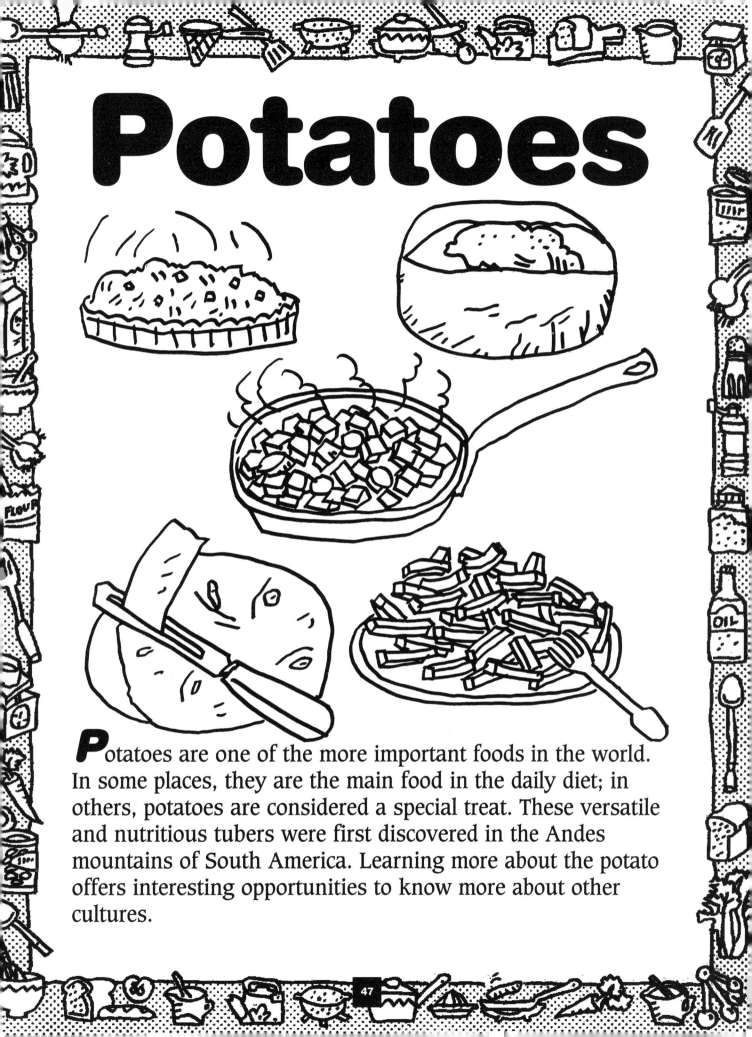

Potatoes are one of the more important foods in the world. In some places, they are the main food in the daily diet; in others, potatoes are considered a special treat. These versatile and nutritious tubers were first discovered in the Andes mountains of South America. Learning more about the potato offers interesting opportunities to know more about other cultures.

Potato Man
Megan McDonald

Grandpa tells a childhood story about the "Potato Man," and how this fruit and vegetable peddler got his name. Discovering how potatoes and other foods were once sold by street vendors is a delightful way to sample a bit of history. Take a look at today's street foods and open air markets found all over the world for another interesting way to learn more about other people and cultures.

As you read the book aloud, focus on where and when this story takes place. Then, use the illustrations to provide a clearer picture of the peddlers, the horse-drawn carriages, the clothing, and the furniture of the times.

After You Read

If possible, pass around a potato for children to examine. Talk about its size, shape, color, eyes, and skin. Help children actually see why the man in the story was called "Potato Man."

Have children name places where potatoes can be purchased. Talk about supermarkets, road-side stands, grocery stores, and so on. Encourage children to think about the different ways they have seen potatoes displayed and sold. Recall how potatoes were sold in the story.

Using an Interactive Chart

To help children appreciate that there are many kinds of potatoes, ask them to think of other words that could replace *Man* in the story. Make an interactive chart with pictures of potatoes and the words *Potato Man* with *Man* replaceable. See how many different words they can name. Write them in the blank space on the word cards and insert in the chart.

Before You Cook

Explain that in different parts of the world, vendors still sell potatoes in the streets. In the highlands of Peru, farmers place blankets on the ground and display baskets of potatoes in the open-air markets. Since there are more than five thousand kinds of potatoes in the Andes, it's easy to imagine why the different sizes, shapes, and colors make this such an interesting sight.

In London, there are colorful potato carts selling hot baked potatoes. These carts look just like the ones used in the days of Queen Victoria. In Belgium, fried potatoes called *frites* (freet) are sold on street corners. They are served in small paper cones with a dab of mayonnaise.

Bring children to a firsthand appreciation of the fact that people serve potatoes in different ways. Each child creates an appetizing dish from a plain baked potato. As children choose ingredients and add toppings, they will discover how availability and people's tastes influence the way foods are prepared.

As You Cook

• Talk about the words *eye* and *skin*. Help children realize that these words have more than one meaning.
• Develop concepts about fractions. Children identify one whole and one half potato.
• Discuss opposites. Focus on cold and hot, hard and soft.
• Invite creative thinking. Children name other toppings that could be put on potatoes.

Stuffed Potatoes
(Serves 8)

Equipment:

knife, paper towels, serving bowls for each of the toppings, real spoons for scooping, real forks for mashing, plastic plates, plastic forks, napkins

Ingredients:

4 large baking potatoes
Tub of margarine
Grated cheddar cheese
Sour cream (or nonfat yogurt)
Cooked chopped broccoli
Bacon bits
Salt and pepper

Teacher:

• Scrub, dry, and pierce the potatoes.
• Bake at 425° for 1 hour.
• Cut each baked potato in half lengthwise.
• Place each of the toppings in a separate bowl and display on the table.
• Hand each child a half potato on a plastic plate.
• Children mash the potato, with or without margarine, then select one or more ingredients to put in the potato or on top.

Book-Related Activities

• **Make a sign for Potato Man's wagon.** As a group, name the items for sale. Use story and picture details for this activity.

• **Children name different dishes:** what Mama might have made with potatoes and what kinds of potatoes they like to eat.

• **Talk about the pomegranate.** Point out that in the story it was also called an Indian Apple. Mention that the word *pomegranate* means "an apple with many seeds." Find out if anyone can tell you why.

• **Look at a cultural beliefs** Pass around a slip of paper that reads: "You will have three times good luck." Recall its significance in this story. Talk about people's beliefs in fortune-telling and fortunes. Help students realize that different cultures have their own ways of predicting the future. As a special treat, why not bring in some fortune cookies. Children can read the fortunes and enjoy the snack.

• Do some journal writing. Remind children to write in their food journals.

Name_____

Make your own potato person. You need:

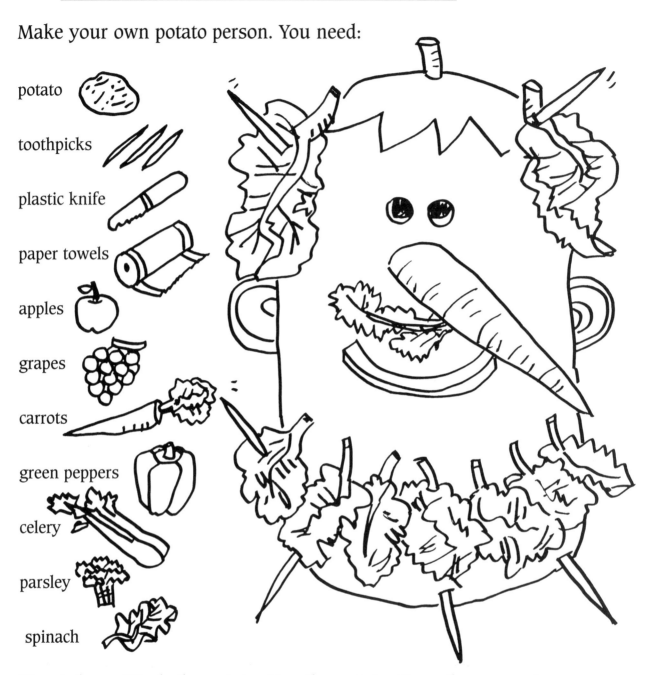

potato

toothpicks

plastic knife

paper towels

apples

grapes

carrots

green peppers

celery

parsley

spinach

Here's how. Wash the potato. Dry the potato. Turn the potato into a person. [Cut fruits and vegetables. Make eyes, a nose, a mouth—cutting pieces, slices, chunks, etc., to make eyes, nose, mouth, feet, hair from fruits and vegetables.] Put the person together. Use toothpicks.

Teacher's Note: Help children understand the concept that although everyone may work with the same foods, each person will create something different. Since potatoes spoil quickly, send them home right away. Encourage children to tell their families the story of Potato Man.

Mrs. Katz and Tush
Patricia Polacco

Read about a special friendship between an old Jewish widow and a young African-American boy; learn about some Jewish customs, traditions, and foods. Get a taste of potato kugel, potato pancakes, gefilte fish, matzoh, and glimpse a Passover Seder.

As you read the book aloud, help children appreciate that there are many kinds of friendships. Skim the book a second time and talk about the different things Mrs. Katz and Larnel did together.

After You Read

Bring some matzoh to class and give everyone a chance to taste it. Have students recall what Mrs. Katz said about matzoh and why she hid a piece of it in her apartment. Explain that the hiding of the matzoh is fun for all the children at a seder. Mention that everyone searches for the piece of matzoh. Usually, only the child that finds it receives a gift.

Ask what else children learned about Passover. Point out that most holidays have special foods associated with them. Help children appreciate what makes matzoh different from other breads. Identify other unfamiliar foods that were mentioned in the story.

Before You Cook

On a map, locate Warsaw, Poland — Mrs. Katz's homeland. You might mention that most of the world's potatoes are grown in Russia. Poland ranks second. Talk about the dishes Mrs. Katz made with potatoes: potato kugel and potato pancakes. Ask children how they know that potato kugel was her specialty. Help children appreciate how much love went into Mrs. Katz's cooking.

Although Mrs. Katz probably grated the potatoes by hand, you can use a food processor to make your own miniature kugels.

Book-Related Activities

• **Learn a Jewish dance.** In the story, Mrs. Katz teaches Larnel a dance from her homeland. If possible, invite a parent or other special guest to teach children the Hora — a simple Jewish dance that's part of many celebrations.

• **Make a list of Yiddish words and expressions used in the story.** Help children use context clues and picture clues to understand what they mean.

• **Locate Warsaw, Poland, Mrs. Katz's homeland, on a map.** Ask the children if any of them were born in another country, or if any of their parents or grandparents were born in another country. See how many different countries are represented in the classroom.

• **Talk about the significance of the phrase "such a person" in this story.** Write that phrase on the chalkboard. Help children appreciate how Mrs. Katz used this expression throughout the book. Find out if any of your children would use "such a person" to describe someone they know.

Mini Kugels
(Makes 12)

Equipment:

potato peeler(s), knife, food processor, 2 large mixing bowls, 1 small bowl, large spoon, plastic measuring cups and spoons, non-stick muffin pan, paper plates, forks, napkins

Ingredients:

5 potatoes, peeled, pared, and grated
1/2 small onion, grated
1/4 cup margarine (1/2 stick)
3 eggs beaten
3 tablespoons matzoh meal
1 teaspoon salt
Cold water (to cover raw potatoes)
Nonstick spray or margarine to grease muffin pan
Sour cream to serve with kugel (optional)

Teacher:

• Grease muffin tin.
• Peel the potatoes. Cut them into small pieces. Place in a large bowl of cold water to cover.
• Grate potatoes in food processor. Place shredded potatoes in bowl of cold water to cover.
• Grate onion in food processor.
• In a small bowl, beat eggs.
• Measure other ingredients.
• Drain shredded potatoes well and squeeze to remove excess liquid.
• Add onion, eggs, margarine, matzoh meal, and salt to potatoes and stir.
• Spoon mixture into muffin tins.
• Bake at 350° for 60 to 70 minutes, until brown.
• Serve warm.

LISTENING/SPEAKING: *A Chant*

Chants are enjoyed all over the world. They motivate children to play with words and help children appreciate the sounds of language. Whenever children gather, they can have fun with chants.

Teach this old favorite:

One potato, two potato,
Three potato, four,
Five potato, six potato,
Seven potato, more.

• Try different versions of this chant.
Use hand motions, clapping, toe tapping, and so on.
• Write different versions of this chant.

APPRECIATING DIFFERENCES

• Read aloud *Mufaro's Beautiful Daughters*: An African Tale, written and illustrated by John Steptoe. This Caldecott Honor book is a wonderful version of the Cinderella story and a delightful way to introduce African culture and yams.
• Read aloud *Princess Furball*, retold by Charlotte Huck. This version of the Cinderella story ties in well with the units on potatoes, soup, bread, and nuts.
• Help children decide how the two stories are alike and how they are different.
• Compare yams and potatoes. Tell how they are alike and how they are different.

Name_____

Tell about Mrs. Katz and you.

Mrs. Katz	Me
Name a holiday that Mrs. Katz likes.	Name a holiday that you like.
Name something special that Mrs. Katz does.	Name something special that you do.
Name a bread that Mrs. Katz eats.	Name a bread that you eat.
Name something Mrs. Katz makes with potatoes.	Name something you make with potatoes.

Teacher's Note: Use this activity to help children discover that people of all ages have things in common.

More Books About Potatoes

Anno's Journey
Mitsumasa Anno

Filled with pleasant surprises, this picture book provides wonderful illustrations of open air markets and street peddlers in European towns and villages.

Odd Potato: A Chanukah Story
Eileen Sherman

A heartwarming story about a young girl who turns an odd potato into a symbol of Chanukah and learns what it means to keep traditions alive.

Jamie O'Rourke and the Big Potato
Tomie dePaola

What happens when the laziest man in Ireland catches a leprechaun? He's offered potato seeds rather than a pot of gold.

Potatoes
Dorothy Turner

This book is filled with all kinds of interesting information about potatoes.

Theme-Related Activities

• **Set up a Potato Market.** Turn a bulletin board into an "open air" market. Once you put up the title, ask children to fill the space with pictures of potatoes and potato dishes. Students can use magazine pictures and labels from cans, packages, and boxes. Everyone should enjoy learning more about potatoes and watching the market grow.

• **Make Potato Sacks.** Have children turn small brown lunch bags into potato sacks. Suggest that they decorate them using crayons, markers, magazine pictures, and so on. These sacks can be used to collect items of interest and to take home theme-related papers and activities.

• **Play games with potatoes.**

Try Hot Potato. You'll need a potato and music. Have players sit in a circle. Start the music and begin passing the "hot potato." Whenever the music stops, the person holding the potato is out. Continue starting and stopping the music, until one winner is left in the circle.

Try Pass the Potato. You'll need two potatoes. Divide the group into two equal teams. The person at the front of each line tucks the potato under his/her chin and passes it to the next in line. See which team gets the potato to the back of the line first.

• **"Dig Up" interesting information about potatoes.** With the group, find out how potatoes grow, where they grow, and the many ways they are used. Ask children to talk to parents and caregivers to see what else they can learn about potatoes.

• **Set up a Potato Stand.** Fill a display table with different kinds of potatoes. Try to include a variety of sizes, shapes, and colors. Pairs of children can pretend to buy and sell potatoes at this classroom market.

• **Write advertisements for potatoes.** Talk about different beliefs and customs. See if children can put them into words or pictures.
Some people believe a potato in your pocket will cure aches and pains.
Some think if you rub a wart with a potato and bury the potato, the wart will go away.
Some believe the best way to cure a sore throat is to put a slice of potato inside a stocking and wear it tied around the neck like a necklace.

• **Take a survey.** Find out which kind of potato is the favorite in your classroom. Choose from mashed potatoes, french fries, potato chips, and baked potatoes.

• **Collect recipes and add to the recipe booklet.** Ask children to bring in recipes for special dishes made with potatoes. Suggest that they include ethnic and/or holiday favorites. Make copies and have children add them to the potato section of their recipe booklets.

Name_____

Grow a potato plant.
You will need:

sweet potato

clear plastic cup

3 toothpicks

water

Try this!

1. Fill container with water — 1/2 to 3/4 full.

2. Stick 3 toothpicks around the middle of the sweet potato.

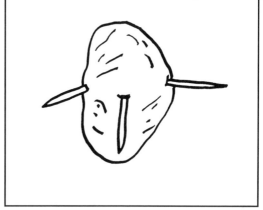

3. Place sweet potato in container, thinner part down—rim of container supports toothpicks.

4. Place the potato near a window.

Teacher's Note: Explain that most potatoes grow underground, but sweet potatoes grow above ground on vines. Encourage children to see what else they can learn about sweet potatoes by watching them grow.

Pancakes

Since the Middle Ages, people have been making pancakes. Today, pancakes are popular all over the world. They are made in different sizes, shapes, and with a wide variety of ingredients. They also provide an appealing way to learn about customs, beliefs, and traditions.

Pancakes for Breakfast
Tomie dePaola

Stir up some interest in pancake-making with Tomie dePaola's wordless book. *Pancakes for Breakfast* provides a delightful picture of what you need to make pancakes.

Help children appreciate how this story is told without words. Tell the story together. Then, call attention to the words used in the pancake recipe, on the ingredients, and on the signs.

After You Read

Have a survey. Children can tell what kind of pancakes they have eaten, and at what times — at breakfast and meals other than breakfast. Talk about things that make pancake-eating special. This may be a good way to discover some interesting traditions that center around pancakes.

Using an Interactive Chart

To help children discover that there are many different kinds of pancakes, create a "pancakes for breakfast" pocket chart. Place blank cards near the chart so that the children can write a word to describe the pancakes—eg., blueberry, silverdollar, etc. Everyone can enjoy seeing how many kinds of pancakes are named.

Before You Cook

Mention that England has a Pancake Day. Also known as Pancake Tuesday, it is celebrated on Shrove Tuesday. This custom began because, traditionally, people gave up butter and eggs for Lent. Making pancakes was a good way to use up all the butter and eggs in the house.

On a map, locate England. Explain that on Pancake Day, in a town called Olney, the women have a pancake race. Each woman carries a frying pan containing one pancake. The women line up in the market square and race across the square to the church door. What makes the race interesting is that the women must flip their pancakes three times before they get to the door. Women in Liberal, Kansas, have a pancake race at exactly the same time. A telephone call at the end of the race determines the winners.

On Pancake Day, English boys and girls gather in the kitchen to eat pancakes. Celebrate pancake day. Make some.

As You Cook

- Define the word *batter*. Help children discover that some words have more than one meaning.
- Call attention to the words *batter* and *butter*. Children decide how the words are alike and how they are different.
- Name the two words that form the compound word *pancake*.
- Discuss the size, the shape, and the thickness of pancakes.
- Decide how a thicker (or thinner) batter will affect the size, the shape, and the thickness of pancakes.

Pancakes
(Makes 15-20 small pancakes)

Equipment:

griddle or electric fry pan, blender, small bowl, fork, spoon, plastic measuring cups and spoons, a ladle, a spatula, paper plates, forks

Ingredients:

1 cup flour
1 egg
1 to 1/4 cups milk
1 tablespoon vegetable oil
2 teaspoons baking powder
1 teaspoon sugar
Non-stick spray or margarine — to grease the griddle
Maple syrup and/or fruit syrup for the pancakes

Teacher:

• Measure the ingredients.
• In a small bowl, beat the egg. Place 1 cup flour, 2 teaspoons baking powder, and 1 teaspoon sugar in the blender. Add the beaten egg, 1 tablespoon oil, and 1 cup milk. Blend. (If batter is too thick, slowly add remaining milk and blend.)
• Grease and heat the griddle. Ladle batter onto hot griddle and cook pancake until bubbles form on top.
• Turn pancake with spatula and brown on other side.
• Serve warm with syrup.

Book-Related Activities

• **Make a personal "Pancakes for Breakfast" picture book.** Each child can draw a picture of family or friends eating pancakes. Children can actually see that everyone has a personal way to enjoy pancakes.

• **Make a list for the old woman in this story.** As a group, skim through the book and recall all the things that she would need to make pancakes.

• **Count your way through this picture book.** Count the pancakes in the stack, the animals in the story, the eggs in the basket, and so on.

• **As a group, rewrite the pancake recipe that is pictured in this book.** Use simple drawings and step-by-step directions, so that beginning readers can follow it. Some children might want to copy the recipe and take it home.

• **Talk about the significance of the saying at the end of the book.**
"If at first you don't succeed...Try, try again."
Decide how this saying applies to cooking and to daily living. You might want to make a copy of this saying and post it in the classroom.

• **Share some interesting beliefs associated with pancakes in England.**
    Some said that if you ate pancakes on Pancake Tuesday and peas the following day, you would have enough money for the year.
    On Pancake Day, farmers threw a pancake to the barnyard rooster. If the rooster ate the pancake, bad luck would follow. However, if the rooster shared the pancake with the hens, the farmer could expect good luck.

• **Mention that in honor of Pancake Day, there is a National Pancake Week.** Have children think of things they could do to stir up interest in pancakes.

Name_____

Here's a poem for you to enjoy.

MIX A PANCAKE

Mix a pancake
Stir a pancake
Pop it in the pan.

Fry a pancake
Toss a pancake
Catch it if you can.

Christina Rosetti

Teacher's Note: Once children learn to read and recite this poem, they can take it home to share.

Pancake Pie

Sven Nordqvist

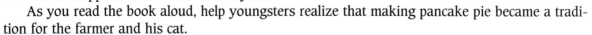

See what a treat pancakes can be in this delightful Swedish tale. *Pancake Pie* is about a farmer who always makes a pancake pie for his cat's birthday, and his cat happens to have three each year.

As you read the book aloud, help youngsters realize that making pancake pie became a tradition for the farmer and his cat.

After You Read

Talk about different ways to make pancakes special. Have children discuss unusual pancakes they have eaten — personalized pancakes, happy-face pancakes, dessert pancakes, and so on.

Describe pancakes from different countries. Mention Swedish pancakes, French crepes, German pancakes, and so on. Help children realize that there are many ways to make and serve pancakes.

Before You Cook

Point out that there are other ways to use pancakes for birthdays. Explain that in Iceland, some people make special pancakes for birthdays. These are called *ponnukokur* (PAHN-er-KER-kuh) . This thin, crepe-like pancake can be covered with fruit preserves (or sugar) and rolled, or folded, into a wedge and served with whipped cream.

After you locate Iceland on a map, make and roll some birthday pancakes.

Book-Related Activities

• **List the ingredients that the farmer needed to make the pancake pie.** Then, think of other things that can be made with milk, sugar, butter, flour, and eggs.

• **Talk about birthday traditions.** Recall how the farmer always makes a pancake pie for cat's birthday. Encourage children to tell about birthday traditions they know. Mention that some Russian people make birthday pies instead of cakes, and that the birthday greeting is written by poking tiny holes into the dough before baking.

• **Act out the Pancake Pie story.** Make sure to include all the obstacles that the farmer and his cat face.

• **Compare *Pancakes for Breakfast* and *Pancake Pie*.** Help children realize that both stories deal with the difficulties of making pancakes.

• **Do some journal writing.** Remind children to include items of interest, observations, and responses to stories, to cooking, and to activities in their food journals.

Ponnukokur

(Makes 20-25 small crepes)

Equipment:

a non-stick pan, large mixing bowl, plastic measuring cups and spoons, small bowl, fork, hand mixer, spatula, ladle, plastic knives, paper plates, napkins

Ingredients:

1 1/2 cups flour
1 tablespoon sugar
1/2 teaspoon baking powder
1/2 teaspoon salt
2 cups milk
2 tablespoons oil
1/2 teaspoon vanilla
2 eggs
Non-stick spray to grease pan
All Fruit ™ spreadable fruit to use for filling. If possible, have two different kinds so that children can choose.

Teacher:

• Mix the 1 1/2 cups flour, 1 tablespoon sugar,1/2 teaspoon baking powder, and 1/2 teaspoon salt in the mixing bowl.
• Add 2 cups milk, 2 tablespoons oil, 1/2 teaspoon vanilla, and 2 eggs. Stir until smooth.
• Grease and heat pan. Ladle a small scoop of batter into the hot pan to make thin, crepe-like pancakes.
• When bubbles appear on top, turn pancakes over. Remove and cool. Then, spread with All Fruit ™ and roll.

LISTENING/STORYTELLING: *A Tall Tale*

Tall tales are stories that are difficult to believe because they are so full of exaggeration. However, many people think that they are just a more interesting way to tell what actually happened.

In the early days of this country, storytelling was one of the most popular forms of entertainment. With a little bit of creativity, people could make any story bigger and better.

When people hear the name Paul Bunyan, they picture a giant lumberjack, a lumber camp, trees, and a blue ox named Babe. But, I picture pancakes — lots and lots and lots of pancakes. Some say that Paul Bunyan was so big that he ate four hundred fifty pancakes a day. And, that was just his breakfast!

In the lumber camp, feeding the men was always a problem. No one could make the food fast enough to satisfy the hungry appetites. Since the lumberjacks' favorite food was hotcakes, they needed a griddle the size of a football field. The only way to grease it was by a team of men skating around with slabs of bacon tied to their feet. And, you wouldn't believe how many cement mixers were used to stir the batter! So, the next time you hear the name Paul Bunyan, think of hotcakes — lots and lots and lots of hotcakes!

Name_____

The farmer made a pancake pie for his cat.
You can make a pancake pie, too.

Who would get your pancake pie?_____

How many pancakes would you use?_____

How would you make your pancake pie?

1. _____

2. _____

3. _____

Show how your pancake pie would look. Draw a picture.

Teacher's Note: As children complete this activity, help them realize that people have different traditions.

• Have children decide what makes a story a tall tale. Ask them to tell about other tall tales they've heard.
• As a group, write a tall tale about pancakes. Call attention to what each person adds to the story.
• Help children realize that there are other names for pancakes. Talk about hotcakes, griddle cakes, flapjacks, and so on.

APPRECIATING DIFFERENCES
• Read aloud *The Gingerbread Boy* by Paul Galdone. Children should enjoy Galdone's version of this children's classic.
• Read aloud *The Pancake* by Anita Lobel. In this old Norse folktale, a runaway pancake is also being chased by hungry pursuers.
• Compare the two stories. Have children decide how they are alike and how they are different.

More Books About Pancakes

Pancakes, Pancakes
Eric Carle

Starting from scratch, Jack helps to gather all the ingredients for breakfast pancakes.

Paul Bunyan: A Tall Tale
Retold and illustrated by Steven Kellogg

In this version of the Paul Bunyan legend, there are tons of flapjacks, barges filled with maple syrup, and a most unusual griddle.

The Wolf's Chicken Stew
Keiko Kasza

A lighthearted story about a wolf determined to fatten up Chicken for a delicious chicken stew. Making one hundred pancakes is just the beginning.

Potato Pancakes All Around: A Hanukkah Tale
Marilyn Hirsh

In this Jewish folktale, a wandering peddler teaches the villagers how to make potato pancakes from a crust of bread.

Fin M'Coul, The Giant of Knockmany Hill
Tomie dePaola

Fin M'Coul is another name that could be associated with pancakes.

Theme-Related Activities

• **Create a Pancake House.** Stock a corner of the room with a plastic mixing bowl, a wooden spoon, plastic measuring cups and spoons, a pan or griddle, a spatula, an apron, and plastic plates and forks. Children can visit the corner and pretend to make, flip, and serve all kinds of pancakes.

• **"Flip" over pancakes.** Provide small lightweight frying pans and small square pot holders. Invite children to pretend that the pot holders are pancakes which they place inside the pan. Suggest that the children try to flip and catch a pancake. Once children have time to practice, they might want to act out the pancake races in England and/or recite the "Mix a Pancake" poem.

• **Make a display,** "The Art of Making Pancakes." As an ongoing activity, ask children to gather magazine pictures of all different kinds of pancakes. Encourage them to find examples of pancakes that are served for breakfast, for lunch or dinner, and for dessert. Display a wide variety of pancakes and include interesting labels or explanations for each. Try to include pictures of French crepes, blintzes filled with cheese, bite-sized Russian blinis with caviar or sour cream, Chinese Moo Shoo Pork, and so on.

• **Watch a Cooking Demonstration.** Invite a class helper to visit and show how to make a specialty pancake. This would be an interesting way to get a taste of Fajitas, blintzes, egg rolls, or some other ethnic pancake.

• **Make a stack of pancakes.** Cut "pancake" circles from oaktag. On each circle, suggest a simple theme-related activity that children can complete independently. Pile the circles on a paper plate at a learning center and encourage children to follow the directions on a pancake of choice.

Examples:
Draw two stacks of pancakes.
Make one stack short.
Describe your favorite pancakes.
Name five things people put on pancakes.

• **Gather pancake recipes.** Ask children to bring in favorites and ethnic specialties. Make copies for children to add to the pancake section of their recipe booklets.

• **Use the Student's Page** to help students create their own recipes for rolled, wedge-shaped, or envelope-style filled pancakes.

Name_____

Make your own recipe card. Choose one. Cut and paste.

1.   1.   1.

2.   2.   2.

3. Rolled Pancake   3. Pancake Wedge   3. Pancake Envelope

_____ **Pancakes**

| Paste the picture of choice here. | This is what you do: _____ |

This is what you do: _____

_____

_____

_____

_____

I Choose_____

_____

You need_____

_____

_____

_____

_____

_____

Teacher's Note: Have children choose one of the three pancake pictures and paste it on the recipe card. Then, they can write their own recipes for pancakes.

65

Beans

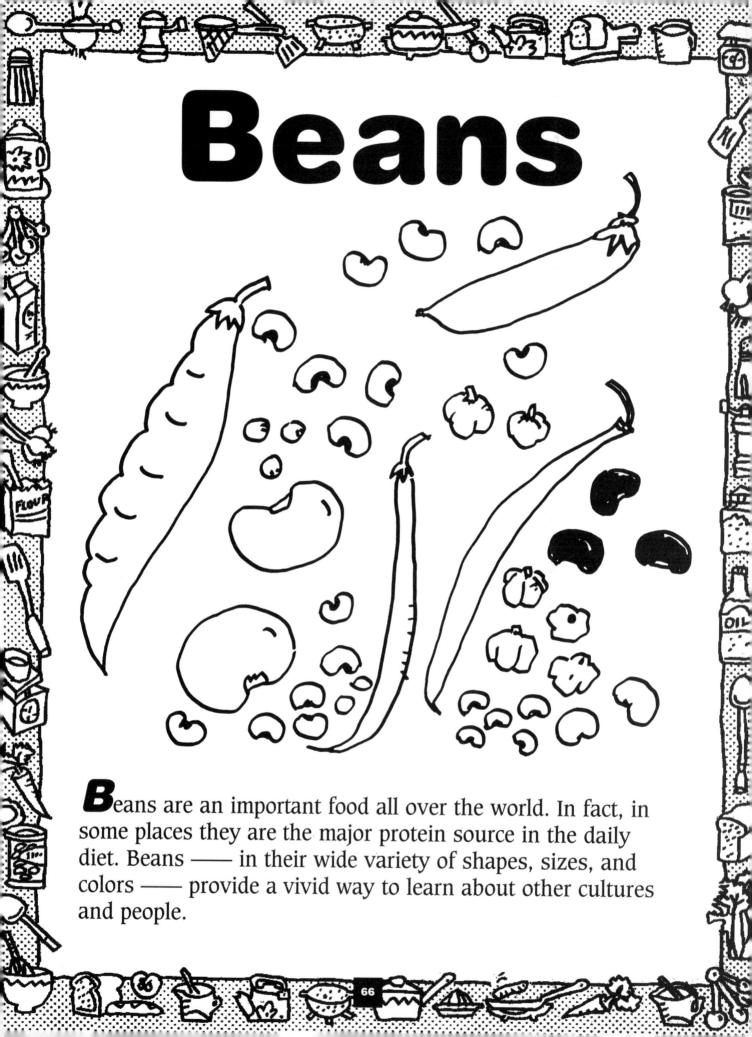

Beans are an important food all over the world. In fact, in some places they are the major protein source in the daily diet. Beans —— in their wide variety of shapes, sizes, and colors —— provide a vivid way to learn about other cultures and people.

Feast for 10
Cathryn Falwell

Follow along as an African-American family shops, cooks, sets the table, and enjoys a feast for ten. This rhyming number book shows how the children choose five kinds of beans in the store and illustrates how a whole family works together.

The first time you read the book aloud, encourage children to listen carefully. As you reread the story, have them join in and add rhyming words and/or number words.

After You Read

Decide why it's important to make a shopping list. Talk about how a list would be helpful to the family in this story. Recall some of the things they bought at the store. Then, make a list. Write the names of the five kinds of beans they needed.

Find out what kinds of beans children might like to buy. Make another list of five kinds of beans. Count the 10 different kinds of beans listed. Then, see how many more beans can be named.

Using an Interactive Chart

To help children understand that groups of every size and kind can make special meals, create an illustrated chart with the words "A Feast for _____" on it. Invite them to complete this phrase using numeral cards and number word cards in many different ways.

Before You Cook

Talk about the size, shape, and color of beans. Mention that besides tasting good, beans also are good for you. Ask what kind of beans (and bean dishes) children have eaten. Describe bean dips, rice and beans, hot dogs and beans, bean tacos, and ethnic favorites.

Pass around pictures of fresh, canned, and dried beans. (Make it clear that the canned beans are cooked and ready to use.) Decide how the beans are different.

Display and count the three cans of beans. Then, use these different kinds of beans to make a colorful Mexican dish, Three-Bean Salad.

As You Cook

• You might have children actually measure the amount of drained beans in each can. One at a time, have them place the drained contents of each can in a measuring cup. Children compare the amount of beans in each can. Find out if they are equal.

• Set aside beans from each can for children to sample. Describe the taste of each bean. See which bean children like the most.

Three-Bean Salad
(For 12)

Equipment:

can opener, a large clear mixing bowl, colander, salad spoons, small bowl, plastic measuring cups and spoons, 3-oz paper cups, plastic forks

Ingredients:

1 large can kidney beans
1 large can green beans
1 large can garbanzo beans
6 tablespoons vinegar
2 tablespoons unflavored oil
1/4 cup water
1 teaspoon sugar
Salt and pepper

Teacher:

• Drain each can of beans and rinse with water.
• Set aside a few beans from each can for children to sample.
• Put the remaining beans in the large bowl.
• In the small bowl, combine 6 tablespoons vinegar, 2 tablespoons oil, 1/4 cup water, and 1 teaspoon sugar. Stir.
• Pour over beans and toss.
• Add salt and pepper.
• Chill and serve.

Book-Related Activities

• **Create a shopping list to go along with this story.** List all the items the family bought...and show how many.

• **Make shopping carts.** Fold a sheet of white paper in half, and seal both sides with a stapler. Cut circles from paper and add the wheels. Bend a long pipe cleaner, and attach the handle. Children can draw lines on the cart to make it look more authentic. They can fill and refill their carts with pictures of beans and other foods they'd like to buy at the grocery store.

• **Print a menu for the "Feast for 10."** Use book details and pictures to decide which foods the family served.

• **Plan a trip to a local supermarket.** Together, locate fresh green beans, jelly beans, dried pinto beans, canned black beans, bean paste, and so on. Children should make their own observations about how food is organized in the store.

• **Create "Feast for 10" picture books.** Number the pages from 1 through 10. Children start with one grocery bag and show, in sequence, the number and the kinds of items they would choose.

Name_____

Tell how many beans are in your salad.

We used ___kinds of beans.   We made ____- Bean Salad.

Make new recipes. Tell what you would add.

I could make ___-bean salad. I would add_____.

I could make ___-bean salad. I would add_____.

Teacher's Note: Children discover that they can easily change the recipe to four- or five-bean salad by adding other kinds of beans.

A BOOK TO READ ALOUD

How My Family Lives in America
Susan Kuklin

Through this series of photo essays, meet and find out how a young Chinese girl lives in America. Discover that she speaks two languages, uses two alphabets, attends two schools, and enjoys both American and Chinese foods.

At this time, read aloud only the last photo essay in the book. (Enjoy the other two children's stories as part of the "Appreciating Differences" section in this unit.) Go through the story a second time, to look at family pictures and discuss interesting details.

After You Read

Take a closer look at the photos of April eating sesame noodles and eating pizza. Call attention to the boxed drink she's having with her Chinese snack, and the pot of tea that's being served with the pizza. Point out that both pictures show how April combines Chinese and American ways.

Ask what else children learned about April. Talk about the different things her family does together. Encourage the children to tell about their own families and decide what ways they may be similar to April's.

Before You Cook

On a map or globe, locate Taiwan and New York. Let children actually see how far it is from one place to the other.

Talk about the kinds of beans people use in China. Mention fresh beans, bean sprouts, and soybeans. Explain that in China and Japan, soybeans are used in different forms because they are high in protein. Tofu is a bean curd cake made from dried soybeans. Soy sauce is also made from soybeans.

Show children how to stir fry, a popular cooking technique used in China. Use two different kinds of beans — fresh beans and soy sauce.

Book-Related Activities

• **Learn how to say two words in Mandarin.** *Baba* (bah-bah) is "daddy" and *mama* (mah-mah) is "mommy." Find out if anyone can teach the class how to say these words in another language.

• **Create a "How My Family Lives in America" bulletin board.** Invite students to bring in and display photos of their families doing special things together. Include a sentence or two with each picture.

• **Post a copy of the old Chinese saying that April mentions.** "The older you are, the wiser you become." After you talk about its meaning, point out that this is a belief shared by many cultures.

• **Talk about Tangram,** the Chinese game that April plays with her family. Supposedly, this game was created in China, four hundred years ago, by a man named Tan. He accidentally dropped his greatest possession — a precious ceramic tile — and it broke into seven pieces. Tan spent the rest of his life trying to put the puzzle back together. Although he wasn't successful, his puzzle game was. It has been passed down from generation to generation.

Stir-Fried String Beans
(For 8-10)

Equipment:

Electric frying pan with lid, large bowl, plastic knives with serrated edges, cutting board(s), slotted spoon, plastic measuring cups and spoons, paper plates, forks

Ingredients:

3 tablespoons oil
1 pound fresh string beans
1 tablespoon soy sauce
1 teaspoon sugar
1 cup water

Teacher:

• Wash string beans and cut off ends. Cut string beans in half.
• Put 2 tablespoons oil in pan. Add string beans and stir fry on medium heat for a minute or two, until oil coats beans.
• Pour 1 cup water in pan, cover, and cook for 8-10 minutes, until beans are tender.
• Remove beans with slotted spoon, and drain liquid from pan. Then, quickly stir fry beans with 1 tablespoon oil,
1 tablespoon soy sauce, and 1 teaspoon sugar.
• Cool slightly and serve.

• **Show children how to make Ba Bao Fan (Eight Treasure Rice).** (*Ba* means "eight" in Chinese.) Invite someone who is Chinese to visit the class and demonstrate making the sweet that's traditional for the Chinese New Year. This colorful dish is made with rice, red bean paste, assorted dried fruits, and pickled vegetables.

LISTENING: *A Holiday*

Explain that Japan has a Bean-Throwing Festival.

According to the lunar calendar, it occurs on the last day of winter. People of all ages throw beans in order to drive away imaginary devils.

Traditionally, the children are asked if they've been good. Of course, they say "yes." Then, in order to bring in good luck for the coming year, and keep away all the bad, the children throw beans as they say:

Oni Wa So To   The devil is going out.
(o-ne wa so to)

Fu Ku Wa Uchi   Fortune should be coming in.
(fu ku wa u-che)

Another way to insure a good year is to eat the number of beans equal to one bean plus your age. Since it is not customary to celebrate birthdays in Japan, everyone becomes one year older around the new year.

Give each child the opportunity calculate how many beans would be eaten if he/she wanted to be sure of a good year.

Name_____

This is how April writes.	This is how I write.
一 *yee* is one	
二 *uhr* is two	
三 *sahn* is three	
四 *suh* is four	
五 *woo* is five	
六 *lyo* is six	

Teacher's Note: Since numbers are such an important part of this unit, children should enjoy learning how to count and write in Chinese.

APPRECIATING DIFFERENCES

• Read aloud the first photo essay in *How My Family Lives in America*. Learn how Sanu, an African-American girl, and her family enjoy their heritage.
• Then, read aloud the second photo essay in this book. Discover how Eric, a Hispanic American, and his family maintain their cultural identity.
• Decide how Sanu's family and Eric's family are alike and how they are different.
• Look at the three recipes in the back of the book. Identify the bean used in each one.

More Books About Beans

Jack and the Beanstalk
Retold and illustrated by Steven Kellogg

    In this version of the classic fairy tale, Jack sells his cow for five beans. Could it be the magic number?

The Stinky Cheese Man and Other Fairly Stupid Tales
Jon Scieska and Lane Smith

    A very unusual book with unique versions of classic fairy tales, including "Jack's Bean Problem."

How a Seed Grows
Helene Jordan

    The book explains how bean seeds that are planted in eggshells grow into plants.

Count Your Way through China
Jim Haskins

    A wonderful way to learn more about Chinese culture and extend the emphasis on numbers and counting.

Theme-Related Activities

• **Celebrate a Bean Feast.** Fill a bulletin board with pictures of all kinds of bean dishes. Show bean soups, dips, casseroles, desserts, and ethnic specialties. Include a sentence or two about each food, to give children a taste of how different cultures use beans.

• **Make Bean Bags.** Use crayons, markers, magazine pictures, and glue to turn small brown lunch bags into Bean Bags. Children can use these bags to collect pictures, recipes, labels, and information about beans.

• **Conduct a Bean Poll.** Explain that long ago, the Greeks and Romans used black and white beans for voting. The white bean was used to cast a "yes" vote; the black bean meant "no." If possible, have some dried black and white beans on hand, and give every child one of each. Plan to vote on something that is important to the group.

• **Make Bean Jars.** Provide baby food jars with lids and a large plastic bowl filled with an assortment of colorful beans.

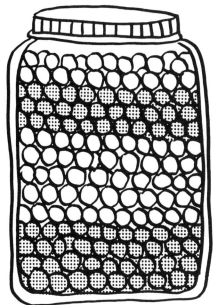

As children fill the small jars with layers of colored beans, they will make their own discoveries about sizes, shapes, colors, and design. You might also suggest that children work in pairs and try to duplicate each other's designs.

• **Hold a Bean Count.** Display a small jar of jellybeans, and invite children to "guess-timate" how many are in the container. Together, count the beans and find out who came the closest.

• **Make Bean Mosaics.** Introduce mosaics — a popular Iranian art form. If possible, show some examples. Explain that first, a design is drawn on paper. Then, the artist places small colored tiles on the design to create a picture. Give children the opportunity to experiment with bean mosaics. Provide white oaktag, glue, crayons, and an assortment of colored beans. Mention that a pitcher is often the subject of a mosaic. (It's also easy to draw and is food-related.) Suggest that everyone make a mosaic pitcher. Develop the concept that although everyone uses the same subject and the same kind of beans, every finished product will be different.

• **Pass around some dried lima beans.** Then, place the beans in a small pot and cover with water. Put the pot in a refrigerator overnight. Check the beans the next day. Notice what happened to the beans and to the water. Encourage children to offer explanations. Then, open a few of the beans and look inside. A magnifying glass might help children detect the beginnings of some sprouts.

• **Collect bean recipes.** Encourage children to bring in ethnic specialties and favorites. Make copies so that children can add them to the bean section of their recipe booklets.

Name_____

Play "Spill the Beans."

Make this.

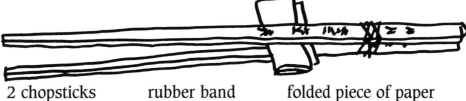

2 chopsticks   rubber band   folded piece of paper

an egg timer

a plastic container

assorted dried beans

Play

1. Spread beans on table.

3. With chopsticks, pick up one bean at a time.

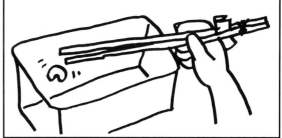

4. Put the bean in the container.

2. Turn over egg timer.

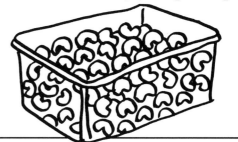

5. See how many you pick up.

Teacher's Note: Children can record the total number of beans, or they can record how many of each color they pick up.

Eggs

Throughout history, eggs have been part of interesting customs, beliefs, traditions, legends, and games. In some cultures, they're even an important art form. People all over the world use, cook, and enjoy eggs in different ways. Learning more about eggs offers interesting opportunities to know more about other cultures.

A BOOK TO READ ALOUD

Rechenka's Eggs
Patricia Polacco

Stir up some interest in eggs and the custom of decorating them. From simple breakfast eggs to spectacular painted eggs, this story is a lovely way to discover the importance of eggs and to get a taste of some Russian traditions.

As you read the story aloud, help children appreciate the beauty of the story and the colorful eggs. Call attention to Russian words, foods, architecture, and celebrations.

After You Read

Talk about the eggs the Russian woman painted for the Easter festival in Moskava. Make sure children realize how delicate the eggshell is, once it is blown. Have children describe their own egg-coloring experiences: Discuss hard boiled eggs and art materials. Children might like to know that egg decorating is an interesting art form in many cultures.

Using an Interactive Chart

• To introduce children to different kinds of eggs, make an interactive chart reading: Rechenka's Eggs! The word *Rechenka* is replaceable. Suggest that children think of words that could replace Rechenka. Find out how many eggs the class names.

Before You Cook

On a map, locate Russia. Talk about how the Russian woman blew out the inside of each egg to use for her breakfast. Name the kinds of eggs she might have made. Recall that painted eggs were part of the holiday celebration. Explain that colorful eggs are also part of the traditional zakuski table in Russia. As part of the first course of a festive meal, a variety of cold salads are served. Russian Egg Salad is a popular favorite.

As You Cook

• Help children identify the parts of an egg. Name the shell, the yolk, and the white of the egg.
• Explain how to make a hard boiled egg. Since the eggs were prepared ahead of time, tell the children what you did.
• Talk about the importance of how food looks. Find out how many children are willing to taste something new, if they like its appearance.

Book-Related Activities

• **Talk about Patricia Polacco.** Tell youngsters that as a child, this author/illustrator loved listening to her grandparents' stories. Explain that Grandma and Grandpa came from Russia. Decide why this information would be of interest. As a group, write your own story about Russia. Include things children learned from this book.

Russian Egg Salad
(Makes 8)

Equipment:

mixing bowl, large spoon, small spoon, cutting board, knife, measuring spoons, platter, small plates, napkins

Ingredients:

4 hard boiled eggs
4 cherry tomatoes
2 tablespoons mayonnaise
1 slice ham
Pinch of salt

Teacher:

• Wash the tomatoes. Cut them in half.
• Chop the ham.
• Wash and peel the eggs. Cut them in half.
• Carefully, scoop the yolk out of the egg. Mix with the chopped ham and 2 tablespoons mayonnaise. Add a pinch of salt.
• Fill the egg whites with the mixture.
• Place a tomato half on top of each egg, and arrange on the platter.

• **Demonstrate how to blow an egg.** Read aloud the description in the story. Then, write simple step-by-step instructions. Mention that you would suggest gently washing and drying the eggshell and sterilizing the needle beforehand. Point out that although blown-out eggshells are very fragile, the artist doesn't have to worry about the egg spoiling.

• **Make a list of different materials that could be used to decorate eggs.** See how many possibilities youngsters can describe.

• **If possible, invite a local artist or art teacher** to visit the classroom and share information about decorating eggs. Children might want to learn about interesting designs and techniques. They might also enjoy seeing a picture of Fabergé eggs — jeweled eggs designed by the Russian goldsmith Carl Fabergé.

• **Ask children about Easter traditions at their homes.** Have them describe special foods and activities.

• **Do some journal writing.** Remind children to write in their food journals.

Name_____

The woman painted eggs. She used different shapes.

stars   flowers   triangles   circles

Make a beautiful egg. Cut out the different shapes and paste them on the egg or draw your own.

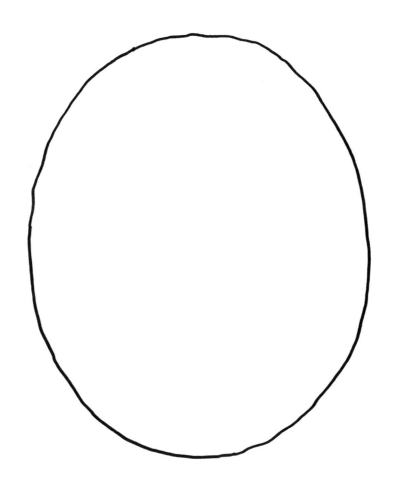

Teacher's Note: To help children appreciate egg decorating as an art form, suggest everyone use the same four shapes to decorate their eggs. Allow time to discover how each egg turns out different.

A BOOK TO READ ALOUD

Just Plain Fancy
Patricia Polacco

Just Plain Fancy is a story about appreciating differences in eggs, in people, and in the ways of the world.

As you read the book aloud, make sure children understand where and when this story takes place. To provide a clearer picture of the Amish ways, go through the book again and talk about the illustrations.

After You Read

Help children appreciate the fact that there are many different kinds of eggs. Talk about the eggs that Naomi collected. Point out what can be learned by examining an eggshell.

Find out how many children have eaten eggs with white shells, with brown shells. Mention that people all over the world eat these kinds of eggs. Explain that in some parts of the world, people eat other kinds of eggs, also. Mention duck eggs, goose eggs, quail eggs, ostrich eggs, and even fish eggs (caviar). Point out that many of these eggs are delicacies.

Before You Cook

On a map, locate Pennsylvania — home of the Amish people. Explain that since the 1700's, these people have lived in this area and maintained their simple lifestyle.

Talk about the meaning of the words *plain* and *fancy*. Help children decide how these terms apply to the way people live, dress, and cook. Ask children to explain the difference between a plain meal and a fancy meal. Then, have children help you turn plain eggs into a fancy omelet.

As You Cook

• Demonstrate how to break an egg. Have children beat the eggs.
• Ask the children to help you figure out how to cut the egg into equal portions.
• Name other fillings that could be used in an omelet.
• Mention that a *frittata* is the Italian version of the omelet. It's made with similar ingredients—some include potatoes and onions—but it is not folded.

Book-Related Activities

• **Plan a book talk.** Mention that Patricia Polacco wrote both *Rechenka's Eggs* and *Just Plain Fancy*. Encourage children to compare the stories and look for similarities and differences.

• **Make a list of Naomi's chores.** Talk about each of her responsibilties. Ask children to tell about their chores at school and outside school. Suggest that each child write about a regular chore.

• **Look at rewards.** Decide what getting a white cap meant to Naomi. Help children appreciate the fact that people receive different kinds of rewards for working hard.

• **Talk about working bees.** Point out that the children in this story were looking forward to the working bee, or frolic. As a group, talk about the merits of working together. Bring out how enjoyable cooking projects have been because many children have been involved.

Omelet
(Serves 4-6)

Equipment:

mixing bowl, fork, 3 small dishes, grater, measuring spoons, non-stick pan, spatula, cutting board(s), knife, plastic knives, paper plates, plastic forks

Ingredients:

4 eggs
1 tablespoon water
2 tablespoons Mozzarella cheese, grated
1 tablespoon finely chopped green pepper
1 tablespoon finely chopped tomatoes
Salt and pepper
Margarine or non-stick spray for pan

Teacher:

• Wash and chop the green pepper and tomatoes. Grate the cheese. Set aside in small dishes.
• In the mixing bowl, beat 4 eggs.
• Add 1 tablespoon water.
• Heat the margarine in the pan. Pour in the egg mixture. Using the spatula, carefully push cooked eggs away from the edges of the pan, so that the uncooked portions will move toward the outside. If necessary, tilt the pan slightly.
• When the eggs are no longer runny, add the cheese, chopped tomatoes, and chopped green pepper.
• Fold the omelet in half by using the spatula.
• Slide the omelet onto a serving plate. Cut into 4 to 6 equal portions.

LISTENING/STORYTELLING: *A Fable*

Help children realize that as long as a story has all the right ingredients, it doesn't matter how long it is. Tell your version of this Aesop's fable, "The Fat Hens."

Once there was a lady farmer who had her own hens. Every day the hens would lay several eggs. But, the woman didn't feel that was enough. So, she decided to give her hens more food. Each day, she gave the hens more and more barley. Eventually, the hens got so fat that they couldn't even lay one egg. That poor woman had less than ever.

• Decide what this story teaches about greed. Help children understand the importance of the message.
• Suggest that children retell this story in their own way...using pictures or simple dialogue.

APPRECIATING DIFFERENCES

• Read aloud *Chicken Sunday* by Patricia Polacco. Help children discover that egg decorating, Easter traditions, and love are the perfect ingredients for another story.
• Reread *Rechenka's Eggs* by Patricia Polacco. Or, have children tell you the story as you turn the pages and show the pictures.
• Compare the two stories. Make a list of how they are alike.

Name_____

Some people make eggshell trees. They decorate eggs.

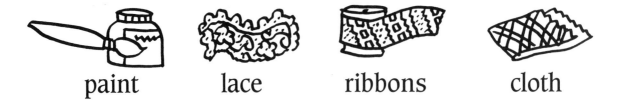

paint   lace   ribbons   cloth

They hang them on a tree. Change these plain eggs into fancy ones. Color the eggs.

Teacher's Note: The tradition of making eggshell trees originated in Europe and was brought to this country by the people who settled in Pennsylvania Dutch country. Use this activity to give children the opportunity to turn plain eggs into fancy ones.

More Books About Eggs

The Most Wonderful Egg in the World

Helme Heine

The King plans to choose the hen that lays the perfect egg. But what happens when he discovers that there is more than one?

Bread and Jam for Frances

Russell Hoban

While the rest of the family is enjoying soft boiled eggs, scrambled eggs, poached eggs, and hard boiled eggs, Frances eats only bread and jam. This old favorite is about trying new things.

The Folks in the Valley:
A Pennsylvania Dutch ABC

Jim Aylesworth

Take a trip to Pennsylvania Dutch Country with this rhyming ABC book. Enjoy a typical day. This book can be a follow up to *Just Plain Fancy*.

The Talking Eggs

Robert D. Sans Souci

This award-winning folktale is about a little magic, a lot of greed, and some very special eggs.

Eggs

Dorothy Turner

This book is filled with interesting information about eggs, foods, and different cultures. It includes some easy-to-follow recipes.

The Cake
That Mack Ate

Rose Robart

A cumulative tale that starts with the egg that went into the cake. This tale even describes the hen that laid the egg and the corn that fed the hen.

Theme-Related Activities

• **Set up a Breakfast Room.** Stock a corner of the classroom with a frying pan, spatula, apron, mixing bowl, fork, plastic plates, cups, forks, and knives. To make it more authentic, include plastic egg-shaped containers (hosiery packaging) and empty egg cartons. Children can pretend to make all kinds of eggs and egg dishes. (Note: If you laminate magazine pictures of different kinds of eggs, children can actually serve colorful items on the plates.)

• **On a Roll.** Egg rolling games and contests are enjoyed by children in many parts of the world. Share information about rolling eggs. Find out what kinds of games children have played with eggs.

Every year children roll eggs on the lawn of the White House. This American tradition was supposedly started in the early 1800's by Dolly Madison.

In Scotland and England, children roll eggs down a hill. The last child holding an unbroken egg is the winner.

In some places, children have egg races in which they use their noses to push the eggs over the finish line. Or, children blow on (or fan) blown-out eggs to move them across the line.

• **Celebrate National Egg Month** (May). Encourage children to think of things they can do to promote interest in eggs as a food, as an important part of many cultures.

• **Develop some concepts about fractions.** EGGS-actly how many eggs are in a dozen, a half dozen, a dozen and a half? For this activity, you need empty egg cartons and egg-shaped forms made of oaktag. Watch children make their own discoveries by placing these specially-made eggs into the empty containers.

• **Plan a different kind of Egg Hunt.** Suggest that children discover how many foods are made with eggs. Encourage them to read package labels and to interview the person who does most of the cooking for them. Set aside time for children to compare their findings.

• **Become EGGSperts.** Suggest that each child learn something important about eggs and share it with the class. From "how to" demonstrations, to interesting information about customs and traditions, to holiday information about eggs and special recipes, each child should have something valuable to show or tell. Award an official (teacher-made) EGGSpert badge to each participant.

• **Add to the recipe book.** Gather recipes for different kinds of egg dishes. Have children bring in favorites and ethnic specialties. Make copies for children to add to the egg section of their recipe booklets.

Name_____

Some people use food to color eggs. You can, too.
You'll need:

What Color?

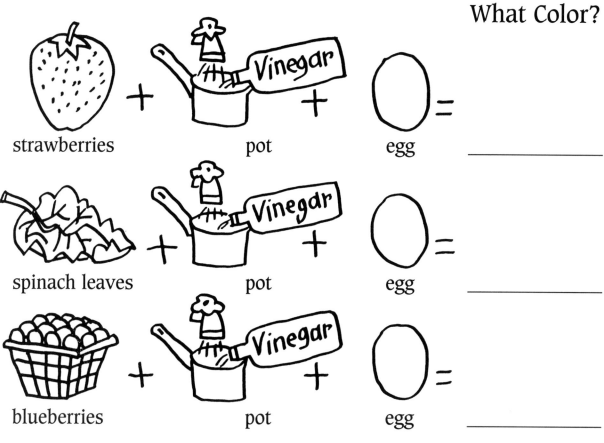

strawberries   pot   egg   _____

spinach leaves   pot   egg   _____

blueberries   pot   egg   _____

Which food would you use?_____

What color is it?_____

Show how your egg would look.

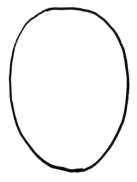

Teacher's Note: To demonstrate how fruits and vegetables can be to used to decorate eggs, have children predict the color that each food will create. Help them appreciate another way to use food in artwork.

Corn

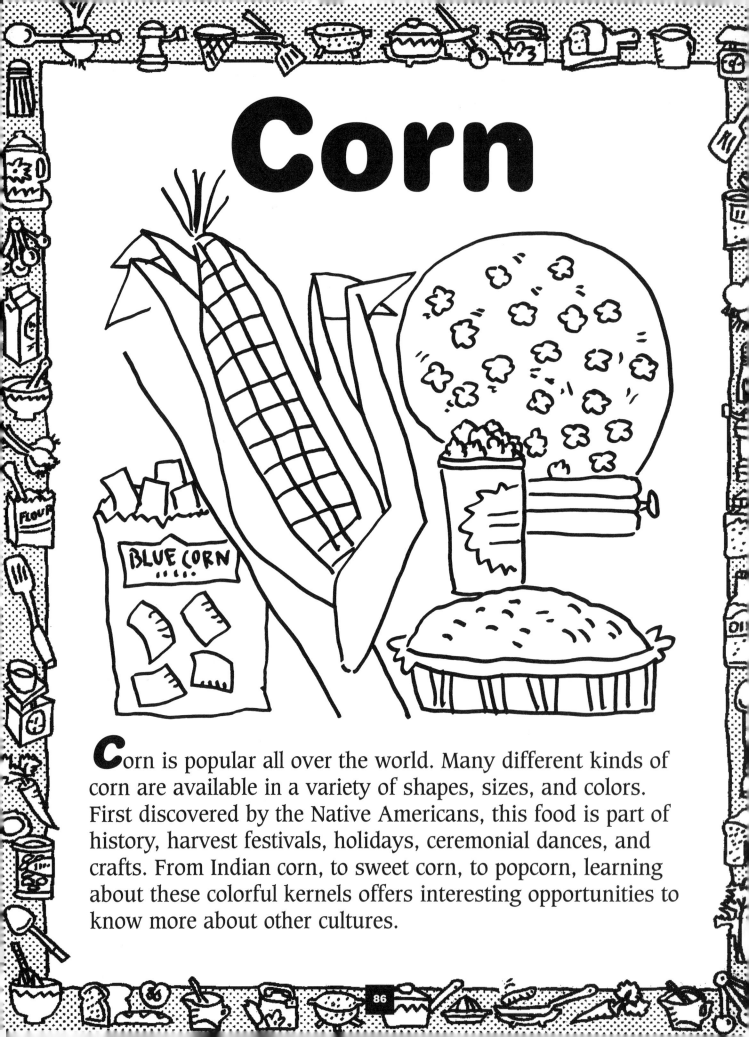

Corn is popular all over the world. Many different kinds of corn are available in a variety of shapes, sizes, and colors. First discovered by the Native Americans, this food is part of history, harvest festivals, holidays, ceremonial dances, and crafts. From Indian corn, to sweet corn, to popcorn, learning about these colorful kernels offers interesting opportunities to know more about other cultures.

Kwanzaa
Deborah M. Newton Chocolate

Develop an appreciation for how different people celebrate holidays. Learn about Kwanzaa, an African-American harvest festival that lasts for seven days. Discover that corn is one of the seven holiday symbols and is used to represent the number of children in each family.

As you read the story aloud, develop the concept that Kwanzaa is a cultural holiday. Use the picture details to focus on customs and traditions that make the celebration special.

After You Read

Pass around an ear of corn. Ask how it is used during Kwanzaa. (Corn is a holiday symbol; it also shows the number of children in a family.) Point out that this is an interesting way to show how special children are.

Examine the ear of corn. Pronounce the Swahili word for corn, *vibunzi* (vee-BOON-zee). Identify the husk, the silk, the cob, and the kernels. Decide why corn is important at a harvest festival. Talk about how to clean, cook, and serve this kind of corn. Think of other things that people do with corn.

Using An Interactive Chart

Make a pocket chart—with picture of black, red, and green straw mat (for Kwanzaa) — pockets to display ears of corn and show "how many children" are in each of the students' families. Chart reads: How many? Make: 8 -10 ears of corn to place in chart.

Children place ears of corn in the corn holder to show how many children are in their own families. As the children make comparisons, they will gain a better understanding of the concepts more, less, and the same.

Before You Cook

Identify the things that make Kwanzaa unique. Discuss the seven principles that came from the harvest festivals in Africa. Point out that like many holidays, Kwanzaa is about families gathering and appreciating what makes them special.

Talk about the *karamu* (kah-RAH-mu), or feast. Recall the different foods that were served. Ask which of those foods would be made with corn. Identify the cornbread. Explain that people in many parts of the world make cornbread. Point out that although everyone starts with cornmeal, other ingredients will not be the same. Even the cornmeal can differ.

As You Cook

• Develop the concept that cornmeal is made from ground corn. Point out that in some parts of the world, people still do this by hand.

• Mention that people make cornbread sweet, salty, or spicy. Have the children share their ideas about how this recipe will taste.

Cornbread
(Serves 12)

Equipment:

2 mixing bowls, plastic measuring cups and spoons, hand mixer, large spoon, baking dish, knife, napkins

Ingredients:

1 1/2 cups all purpose flour
1/2 cup cornmeal
1 tablespoon baking powder
1/2 teaspoon salt
1/2 cup margarine (l stick)
1/2 cup sugar
2 eggs
1 cup milk
Non-stick spray or margarine to grease baking dish

Teacher:

• Grease baking dish.
• Combine 1/2 cup cornmeal, 1 1/2 cups flour, 1 tablespoon baking powder, and 1 teaspoon salt in mixing bowl. Set aside.
• In another mixing bowl, blend 1/2 cup margarine and 1/2 cup sugar with hand mixer.
• Add the 2 eggs and 1 cup milk to the margarine and sugar. Mix well.
• Gradually add the dry ingredients and stir until there are no traces of the dry ingredients.
• Pour into the greased baking dish. Bake at 400° for 20-25 minutes until golden brown.

Book-Related Activities

• **Locate Africa on a map or globe.** Call attention to its size. Point out that it's one of the largest continents. Help children realize that many different kinds of people live in Africa. Emphasize that they all live in different ways.

• **Count** the Kwanzaa symbols, the Kwanzaa principles, the candles in the *kinara*, and the letters in the word *Kwanzaa*. Talk about the significance of the number seven.

• **Explain how Kwanzaa began.** Talk about Dr. Maulana Karenga, the African-American who was responsible for its creation. Mention that he wanted his people to know more about their history and to be proud of their past. Discuss the Kwanzaa principles and what people of every culture can learn from them.

• **Invite a special visitor.** If possible, contact a local cultural group. Invite a representative to visit the class to talk about Kwanzaa, or African foods, clothing, and customs.

• **Learn words in Swahili.** Make pictionaries. Have children write and illustrate key words like *karamu* (feast), *bendera* (flag), *mkeka* (straw mat), *kinara* (candle holder), and *vibunzi* (ear of corn). Use the book to help with pronunciations.

• **Make Kwanzaa placemats.** Mention the African custom of making things by hand. Recall how the the *mkeka*, or straw mat, was woven. Teach children how to weave their own mats. Use black paper, with one red and green strip.

Name_____

Get the table ready for Kwanzaa. Check ✔ the list below.

❑ Draw candles in the candleholder.

❑ Draw fruits and vegetables in the basket.

❑ What fruits and vegetables will you draw? _____

_____

_____

_____

Teacher's Note: As children complete this activity, they will become more familiar with the symbols of Kwanzaa and gain a better understanding of how families prepare for the holiday.

How Two-Feather Was Saved from Loneliness: An Abenaki Legend

C. J. Taylor

Find out how important corn was to Native Americans. Use this Abenaki legend to show how one tribe explains the way that fire, corn, and community living began.

As you read the story aloud, make sure children understand where and when this story takes place. Go through the book a second time to enjoy the artwork. See if children notice the illustrations signed by the author/illustrator.

After You Read

Discuss why learning to make a fire was so significant. Talk about how it was used to clear the land. Think of other ways that fire would be of use to Two-Feather.

Decide how corn changed Two Feather's life. Talk about how planting and growing crops became the focus of daily life. Explain that people also had to learn how to use the corn. Develop this concept: As Native Americans learned how to plant, cultivate, harvest, and use corn, this food became a part of their history and culture.

Before You Cook

Pass around some popcorn kernels. Introduce another kind of corn grown and used by Native Americans. Explain that long ago, people believed that demons lived inside the kernels. Whenever the demons were heated in a fire, they'd blow up in anger —— and pop!

Mention that Native Americans taught the Pilgrims how to grow and use many foods—including popcorn. They brought bags of it to the first Thanksgiving feast and used earthen jars to show the children how to make popcorn. Then, they poured maple syrup over the popped corn to create sweet treats.

As You Cook

• Have children predict what will happen to the kernels. Ask them to give their own explanations for why it pops.
• Use all five senses to describe the popcorn.
• Explain why popcorn pops. Mention that each kernel contains moisture. When heated, this moisture becomes steam. Steam builds up pressure; when it explodes, Pop!
• Point out the kernels that never pop. Discuss why this would happen.
• Describe different ways Native Americans popped corn. Mention that they placed kernels on hot coals, on stones in a fire, or on hot sand.
• Determine where real maple syrup comes from. Develop the concept that Native Americans learned to use what was available to them.

Book-Related Activities

• **Compare two harvest festivals.** Write the names of two harvest festivals—Kwanzaa and Thanksgiving. Decide how these holidays are similar. Make a list.

Popcorn *Native American Style*
(Makes 22 half-cup servings)

Equipment:

hot air popper, plastic measuring cup, 2 large bowls, ladle, paper plates, napkins

Ingredients:

1/2 cup popcorn kernels
Maple syrup

Teacher:

• Measure l/2 cup popcorn kernels. Pour into hot air popper.
• Fill large bowls with popped corn.
• On each plate, place l/2 cup popcorn and a pool of maple syrup for dipping.
Children can enjoy getting a taste of the popcorn served at the first Thanksgiving.

• **Discuss holiday symbols.** Talk about how ears of corn are used for Kwanzaa. Name the kinds of corn often used for Thanksgiving decorations — Indian corn and cornstalks. Find out what other holidays children associate with corn.

• **Survey corn snacks.** Besides being one of the most popular snacks, popcorn is also good for you. Have children talk about different kinds of corn snacks they like to eat. Encourage them to bring in package labels. Show children how to read and interpret this information. Help them decide which snacks are healthy choices.

• **Make a popcorn book for National Popcorn Month** (October). Fill the book with interesting ways to serve popcorn. To get started, mention that Native Americans taught the Pilgrims how to make and eat popcorn. Help children appreciate the fact that the Pilgrims then had to think of their own ways to use this new food. Mention that the colonists served it with cream and sugar for breakfast and put it in soup to make popcorn soup. Suggest that children think of new ways to serve popcorn. Have them write simple recipes for this book.

• **Invite a special guest.** In some areas, Native American cultural organization have speakers and/or performers that will visit the classroom. If possible, make arrangements for a guest to talk about how different kinds of corn are used for ceremonial corn dances, drying corn, using corn for crafts.

LISTENING/SPEAKING: *A Poem*

Do this popcorn rap:

Pop, pop, popcorn,
popping in the pot,
pop, pop, popcorn,
eat it while it's hot!

Pop, pop, popcorn,
butter on the top,
when I eat popcorn,
I can't stop!

• Encourage children to write their own popcorn poems. Fill the room with some original sounds.

Name_____

Native Americans made popcorn. We made popcorn, too.

They used	We used
What they put on popcorn	**What we put on popcorn**
Why they thought popcorn popped	**Why I think popcorn pops**
_____ _____ _____ _____	_____ _____ _____ _____

Teacher's Note: This activity can help focus on the importance of respecting other people's beliefs.

APPRECIATING DIFFERENCES

• Share the family pictures in the book *Family Pictures/Cuadros de Familia* by Carmen Lomas Garza. Enjoy the art and food-related scenes. Focus on Mexican customs, traditions, and foods.

• Read aloud the section "Making Tamales." Talk about the process of making tamales and the fact that the whole family participates.

• Have children predict what happens to the corn husks when they are soaked in tubs of water. Discuss why the corn husks must be soft.

• Discuss the advantages of preparing food together. Then, use the picture clues to tell how to make tamales — step-by-step.

• Reread the "Making Tamales" section in English and in Spanish. Talk about how different the languages sound. You may wish to mention that in many families, more than one language is spoken.

More Books About Corn

The Popcorn Book
Tomie dePaola

Here's an old favorite that provides fascinating facts about the origin of popcorn and even includes a few recipes.

Corn Is Maize: The Gift of the Indians
Aliki

This read-and-let's-find-out book shows how Native Americans planted, cultivated, harvested, and used corn.

Working Cotton
Sherley Anne Williams

A 1993 Caldecott Honor book about an African-American family working in the cotton fields and eating cornbread and greens for lunch.

Alligator Arrives with Apples: A Potluck Alphabet Feast
Crescent Dragonwagon

A delightful alphabet book about a most unusual Thanksgiving feast — and an enjoyable way to prepare for a holiday.

Too Many Tamales
Gary Soto

A nice way to introduce Hispanic culture, talk about Christmas, and learn the importance of making tamales.

Victory Garden: Alphabet Book
Jerry Pallotta and Bob Thomson

A wonderful alphabet book with pictures of Indian corn, popcorn, Quicksilver(white corn), and unfamiliar crops grown around the world.

Moon Mother: A Native American Tale
Ed Young

Share another Native American tale and learn more about their culture and art.

Theme-Related Activities

• **Create a CORN-meal bulletin board.** Ask children to help fill the board with pictures of all kinds of corn dishes. Show tortillas, tacos, tamales, succotash, spoonbread, corn pudding, and so on. Label the pictures, and include a sentence or two about each dish.

• **Make Popcorn Bags.** Use crayons and markers to turn small brown lunch bags into storage bags. Since popcorn is usually such a popular subject, encourage children to gather their own pictures, words, fascinating facts, and recipes. Some children might also want to do a popcorn survey. Have them ask family and friends when they eat popcorn, where they eat popcorn, and what kind they like best.

• **Create a CORNucopica poster.** Since the horn of plenty is a symbol associated with the harvest, why not fill it with pictures of different kinds of corn and corn products? Suggest that children use magazine pictures, coupon fliers, and labels from packages to find corn oil, corn syrup, cornstarch, corn chips, corn cereals, and so on.

• **Conduct a Taste Test.** Sample 3 or 4 different brands of corn chips or corn cereals. Have each child decide which one tastes the best, which one looks the most appetizing, and which has the most appealing packaging. Show children how to compare their findings; tally the results.

• **Display a big book atlas.** Use *It's a Big Big World Atlas* (Tormont Publications) and ask children to find places where corn grows. By making their own discoveries, children can more easily see why corn is so important to Native Americans, Mexicans, South Americans, and so on. Point out the corn belt in the Midwest. Help children understand that people use what's available to them.

• **Hold a CORNfest.** With the help of a few parents, plan a Mexican feast. Ask volunteers to prepare nachos, mini tacos, tortillas, salsa and chips, and other popular corn dishes. Request that others provide the paper goods. Besides having children sample the foods, you might want to play Cakewalk — the game that was described in the book *Family Pictures*.

• **Explore corn husks.** Mention that in addition to finding different ways to use corn, people also thought of ways to use the husks. Point out that the Native Americans used the husks to make mats, baskets, clotheslines, baby hammocks, and dolls. Recall how the Mexican family used the husks to make tamales. Encourage children to find out about other things people do with corn husks. Suggest that they talk to family and friends.

• **Gather different kinds of corn recipes.** Ask children to collect favorites and/or special holiday dishes. Make copies so that children can include them in the corn section of their recipe booklets.

Name_____

A. People give gifts for Kwanzaa. A book is always one of the gifts. Tell about a book you would give. Write a "recipe" for a favorite book.

B. My "Recipe" for a Good Book

by _____

C. To make a book you need a story. Write or draw what your story is about.

D. What is the name of your story?

_____

Teacher's Note: As children write a different kind of recipe, point out that a book is a special gift for Kwanzaa and for all kinds of holidays in which gifts are given.

Nuts

Nuts come in different shapes, sizes, and colors. Some grow on trees, others on plants. People of all cultures have found ways to cook and use nuts, from coconuts, to peanuts, to gingko nuts. Whether nuts are part of games, crafts, customs, or traditions, learning about them carries opportunities to know more about other cultures.

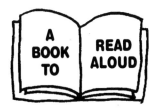

A BOOK TO READ ALOUD

Chicka Chicka Boom Boom

Bill Martin, Jr. and John Archambault

Make time to climb up a coconut tree with A, B, C, D, and E! This rhyming chant is a colorful way to introduce children to palm trees, coconuts, tropical flavors, and the letters of the alphabet.

As you read the book aloud, help children appreciate how playful the text is. Reread the book and ask children to chime in with " Chicka chicka boom boom."

After You Read

Bring a real coconut to class. Have children touch it, shake it, examine it, and predict what's inside. As a group, write a complete description of this unusual-looking nut. Then, think of ways to crack it open.

Since cracking a coconut is difficult, bring in a coconut that's already been opened. After children have had a chance to examine it, give everyone a taste of the white meat. Mention that the coconut milk in a ripe coconut is tasteless and should be discarded. It's the green coconuts in tropical countries that contain the milk that you drink.

Using An Interactive Chart

Create a pocket chart containing a coconut tree and a phrase similar to the one in the book and two alphabet cards for each letter of the alphabet. To help children appreciate the sounds and the rhythm of the language, have them work with the alphabet cards to create a variety of rhymes. See how many different verses they can create.

Before You Cook

Name things that grow on trees. Help children realize that certain trees grow in different parts of the world. Point out that palm trees grow in warm tropical climates. On a map, locate places where these trees can be found.

In some parts of the world, the coconut palm is known as the "tree of life." The actual coconut is an important part of the daily diet. Every other part of this tree is also used.

A simple way of enjoying coconut is to make Ambrosia. The word means "food of the Greek and Roman Gods." According to Roman and Greek mythology, eating this dish would ensure immortality. Point out that there are many different recipes for Ambrosia. Much depends on the fruit available and the people making it.

As You Cook

• Have each child taste a slice of mandarin orange. Children can make comparisons with the kinds of oranges they usually eat.
• If any children have eaten fresh pineapple, have them describe how it looks and tastes.
• Call attention to the colors of pineapples, oranges, coconuts. Decide how mixing different colors makes food more appealing.

Ambrosia
(Serves 8-10)

Equipment:

a large clear bowl, plastic measuring cups and spoons, can opener, serving spoon, 3-oz paper cups, spoons

Ingredients:

2 cups pineapple chunks (1 large can packed in natural juice)
2 cups mandarin oranges (two 11 oz cans)
1 cup shredded coconut
1 cup mini marshmallows
1/2 cup sour cream

Teacher:

• Drain the pineapple chunks and the mandarin oranges.
• Set aside 1/2 cup oranges for tasting and decorating.
• In large bowl, mix pineapple chunks and mandarin oranges.
• Add 1 cup shredded coconut and 1 cup mini marshmallows and mix.
• Then, add 1/2 cup sour cream and blend together.
• As an added touch, place mandarin oranges in a pattern across the top.

Book-Related Activities

• **Listen to the *Chicka Chicka Boom Boom* cassette.** This story is available with an accompanying tape. One side of the tape is narrated by John Archambault (the story's co-author) and the other is performed by singer Ray Charles. If possible, give children the opportunity to enjoy the sounds of both versions.

• **Enjoy the tropical flavor of this book** by focusing on Lois Ehlert's artwork and use of color. Encourage children to use colorful construction paper, scissors, and glue to create their own "tropical settings."

• **Make a list of ways to get a coconut down from a tree.** Help children discover that there is more than one possibility. Point out that the easiest way is to simply wait for them to fall off the tree. Mention that in some parts of the world, agile boys or young men actually climb the tree and cut down the nuts with a machete or bolo. Have children imagine the sounds the nuts make as they hit the ground.

• **Explore uses of the coconut.** "There are as many uses for the coconut as there are days in the year." (Indonesian saying) Help children appreciate the many ways to use a coconut. Encourage children to tell what they know about the uses of coconut. Discover how different cultures use this nut, and talk about the ethnic foods that have coconut in them.

• **Grow a coconut tree bulletin board.** Use construction paper to design a simple coconut palm. Invite children to fill the tree with information about coconuts. Suggest that children gather facts, pictures, product labels, and recipes and place them on display.

Name_____

We made Ambrosia. You can, too.

Ambrosia

You need:
_____
_____
_____
_____
_____
_____
_____
_____

Recipe:
First,
_____
_____

Next,
_____
_____

Then,
_____
_____

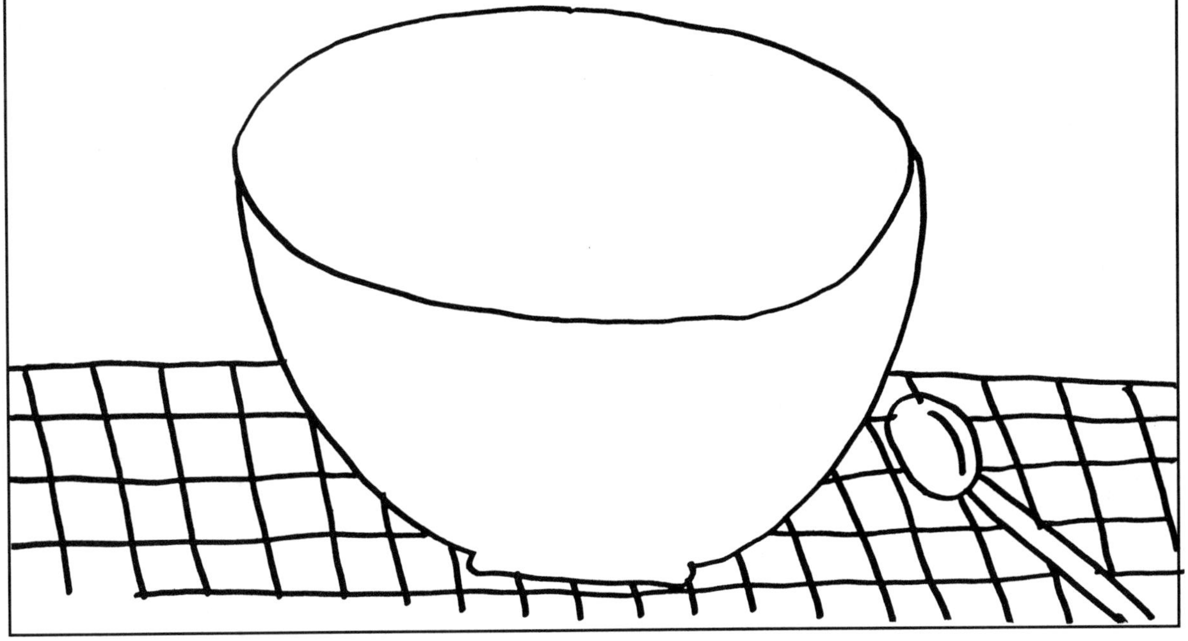

Teacher's Note: To encourage children to experiment with food, have them create their own fruit and nut combinations.

The Village of Round and Square Houses

Ann Grifalconi

*I*n a small African Village, the women live in round houses and the men live in square ones. Find out why. At the same time, get a taste of another culture and some interesting foods such as fou-fou and groundnut stew.

The first time you read the book aloud, make sure children realize that the story is being told from a young girl's point of view. As you reread the book, use the illustrations to learn more about the villager's food, clothing, and way of life.

After You Read

Pass around some peanuts. As children examine them, talk about the size, the shape, and the color. Suggest that children open the nuts and take a taste. Help children realize how easy these nuts are to open. Compare this to opening a coconut and to opening other kinds of nuts.

Have children discuss when and in what form children have eaten peanuts. Encourage individuals to tell about ethnic dishes prepared with peanuts. Develop the concept that there are many different ways to enjoy peanuts.

Before You Cook

On a map, help children locate Africa. Mention that in Africa, peanuts are called groundnuts. See who remembers the groundnut dish described in the book (groundnut stew.) Help children realize that people of different cultures use peanuts in different ways.

Book-Related Activities

• **Have a classical peanut hunt and make a pictograph.** Bring in a bag of peanuts (in shells). Hide them around the classroom or in a small area outdoors. Send children on a peanut hunt. Hand out paper cups. See how many peanuts each child can find.

• **Learn about George Washington Carver.** This famous African-American scientist is known as the king of the peanut. Because of his work, hundreds of products were made from peanuts. You might want to read aloud the book *George Washington Carver: Plant Doctor* mentioned in the "More Books" section of this unit. Ask each child to write something about the man and his work.

• **Have a different kind of peanut hunt.** After talking about George Washington Carver and his work, ask children to help you find products that are made with peanuts. Suggest that children read all kinds of labels (soap, ink, oil, cream, etc.) and make their own scientific discoveries. Have them find out which products are made with peanuts.

• **Make a book about peanuts.** You can make this a group effort. Develop the concept that there are other names for peanuts (groundnuts, goobers, goober peas, ground peas, pindas). Find out how peanuts grow (underground) where peanuts grow, and the many ways to use peanuts.

• **Talk about the foods described in this story.** Recall how the village children helped with cooking and serving. Make a list of all the chores they did. Encourage children to tell how they help or might help at home. Look for similarities and differences.

A Groundnut Treat
(Serves 8)

Equipment:

an electric frying pan, knife,
3 small bowls, large spoon,
plastic measuring cups and spoons,
small paper plates and plastic forks.

Ingredients:

2 cups thin spaghetti, broken into
pieces, 2 T oil, 2 cups hot water,
1/4 cup raisins, 1/4 cup chopped
dates, 1/4 cup peanuts,
1/4 cup sugar

Teacher:

• Break the spaghetti into short pieces.
• Chop 1/4 cup dates. Measure 1/4 cup raisins and
1/4 cup peanuts and set aside.
• Heat 2 T oil in electric frying pan. Add 2 cups
broken spaghetti and stir until lightly brown.
• Pour in 2 cups hot water, chopped dates, raisins,
peanuts, and 1/4 cup sugar.
• Cover and cook for abut 10 minutes, until all
water is absorbed.
• Serve warm.

LISTENING/STORYTELLING: *A Fable*

Aesop's Fables are teaching tales that have been retold so many times, in so many parts of the world, that they have become an important part of children's literature everywhere.

Share one version of Aesop's "The Walnut Tree."

Along the side of the road, stood a big walnut tree. The tree was filled with walnuts. As people passed by, they would throw sticks and stones at the branches. It seemed like the most logical way to get nuts from the tree. But, the tree didn't think so. "How could they do this to me?" cried the tree. "The same people that enjoy my fruit, think nothing of throwing things at me and insulting me."

• Have children discuss what they think this fable teaches. Develop the concept that people aren't always grateful.
• Think of other ways to get the walnuts down from the tree. Recall children's earlier suggestions for getting coconuts down from trees.
• Use this fable to focus on environmental issues. Talk about the importance of people caring for natural resources.

APPRECIATING DIFFERENCES

• Read aloud *Lon Po Po: A Red Riding Hood Story from China* by Ed Young. In this Caldecott Medal winner, three children use a gingko tree and gingko nuts to outsmart the wolf. Share that *Po Po* means "Granny," and that *Lon Po Po* means "Granny Wolf" in Chinese.

Name_____

Make one of the round houses. Cut and paste.

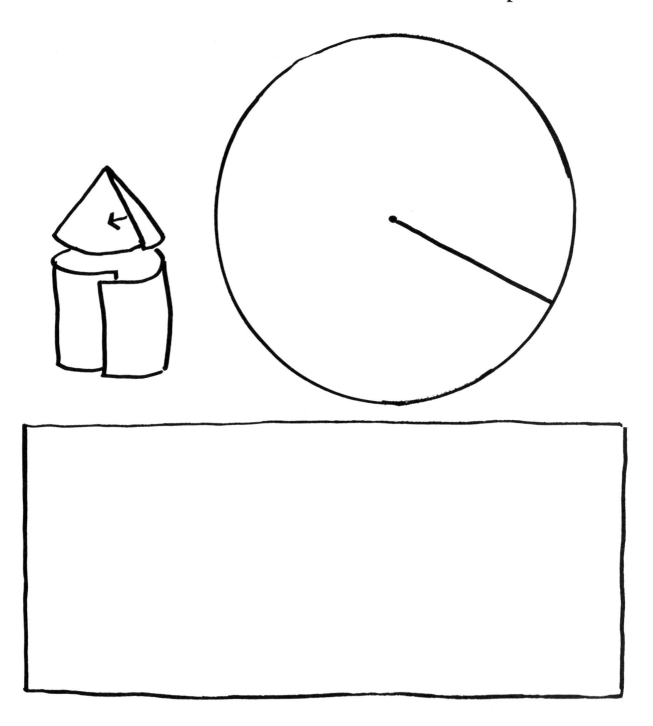

Teacher's Note: As children cut and paste, they should recall that the round house is where the woman and children lived and prepared the food. Suggest that children show these houses as they tell this story at home.

• Read aloud *Little Red Riding Hood* by Trina Schart Hyman. This is a beautifully illustrated version of the German fairy tale.
• Decide how the two stories are alike and how they are different.
• Mention that Ed Young, the author/illustrator, was born and raised in China. Determine why this information could be of interest to readers.
• Learn more about gingko trees and gingko nuts. Explain that the tree is a large ornamental tree that is native to China and the small oval shaped nuts are used in Asian cooking. The nut, shelled and canned, can be bought in a Chinese market.

More Books About Nuts

George Washington Carver: Plant Doctor

Mirna Benitez

Use this biography to introduce a famous African-American and to provide interesting information about the peanut.

Peanut Butter and Jelly

Nadine Bernard Westcott

With its rhyming text and suggested hand and foot motions, this is a delightful way to discover how to make a peanut butter and jelly sandwich.

Nuts to You

Lois Ehlert

Lois Ehlert's simple text and colorful art add to this delightful story about nuts and a squirrel.

The Tale of Squirrel Nutkin

Beatrix Potter

This tale, by the popular English author, should be read aloud and shared.

My World & Globe: An Interactive First Book of Geography

Ira Wolfman

This book can serve as an introductory guide for anyone interested in learning more about places covered in this unit.

Theme-Related Activities

• **Create an "In a Nutshell" bulletin board.** Ask children to help gather pictures of all kinds of nuts. Along with each picture, include its name and an interesting fact. See how many different kinds of nuts children can gather.

• **Set up a "Nuts...About You" Table.** Suggest that children help fill a display table with samples of a variety of nuts. Do include the name of each nut. Then, encourage children to visit the table and count the nuts, describe the nuts, notice likenesses and differences, group them according to size, shape, color, and so on.

• **Plan a tasting party.** With the help of parents, put together an interesting assortment — 4 or 5 kinds — of nuts for children to try. Then, suggest that children list the nuts in order, from the one they liked most to the one they liked least.

• **Enjoy the nursery rhyme, "My Little Nut Tree."** Bring in some nutmeg and give children the opportunity to smell it. Explain that nutmeg is a nutlike seed that's used as a spice in cooking. Children can find out if and how nutmeg is used at home.

MY LITTLE NUT TREE

I had a little nut tree,
 Nothing would it bear
 But a silver nutmeg
 And a golden pear;
The King of Spain's daughter
 Came to visit me,
 And all for the sake
 Of my little nut tree.

• **Learn how to use a nutcracker.**
With the group, write instructions for
how to use it. Ask children to describe
nutcrackers they have seen or used.
Have children design their own nutcrackers using paper and crayons.
Find out how many children are familiar with the story of the Nutcracker. If
possible, plan to see a production of
this holiday favorite.

• **Plan a "Nuts About the Holidays"
project.** Since nuts are part of many
traditional holiday celebrations, share
some bits and pieces with the class.

Gok Jai is a traditional sweet prepared for the Chinese New Year. For this special Chinese pastry,
shredded coconut and peanuts are mixed with sesame seeds and brown sugar, wrapped in a won-
ton skin, and then fried in oil.

On Hanukkah, children play with a four-sided top called a dreidel. If the dreidel lands on the
Hebrew letter *gimel*, that player wins all the nuts that are in the pot.

Gather interesting information about nuts. With the group, find out how nuts are used in various
holiday celebrations. Encourage children from different ethnic backgrounds to tell about their own
experiences. Also, suggest that students ask parents and relatives about special nut dishes.
Children share their information by writing a class newsletter.

• **Collect different kinds of nut recipes.** Encourage children to bring in favorite and/or ethnic
recipes. Help children discover that nuts can be used in soups, main dishes, sandwiches, salads,
drinks, and so on. Make copies of the recipes for children to add to the nuts section of their recipe
booklets.

Name_____

TAKING COCONUTS
A game from New Guinea

You Need: chalk, 5 coconuts, 4 players. **Draw:** One big circle with 4 small circles around it.

How To Play:
Take one nut at a time.
Place it in your circle.
Try to get 3.

Teacher's Note: Since players can take a nut from any one of the circles, they will quickly discover that this is a different kind of game. There is no winner. The game is played for fun, and it ends when everyone has had enough.

Dear Parents,

Our class will be getting a taste of the world by learning about many different foods. As part of each unit, we will plan several cooking projects. You can help. Would you be willing to:

❑ send in several ingredients for our next project?
❑ come to class and help us with the cooking?
❑ cook and send in an ethnic dish for us to sample?
❑ other?

Please let us know how you would like to contribute.

Thank you,

_____

_____

_____

Dear Parents,

We have a cooking project scheduled for _____.
                                          (day, date)
We need _____.
Can you contribute these ingredients? _____
Can you join us? _____
R.S.V.P. by returning this note with your contribution of food.

Thank you,

Recipe Card for gathering recipes

Recipe
Serves _____

For:

_____

_____

From the kitchen of

_____

Equipment:

_____

_____

_____

_____

_____

_____

Ingredients:

_____

_____

_____

_____

_____

_____

How to make:

_____

_____

_____

_____

_____

3.

How to

_____
_____
_____
_____
_____
_____

2.

You need

_____
_____
_____
_____
_____
_____

Draw what your recipe
will look like.

4.

**A
Mini-Cookbook**

Recipe for

_____
_____

by

_____

1.

Teacer's Note: This one is for children. They can write their own simple recipes and fold them into mini cookbooks)

Bibliography

Soup

BOOKS TO READ ALOUD

*Sendak, Maurice *Chicken Soup with Rice* (HarperCollins Children's Books, 1962)

*Ehlert, Lois *Growing Vegetable Soup* (Harcourt Brace Jovanovich, 1987)

LISTENING...A FABLE

*Anno, Mitsumasa *Anno's Aesop* (Orchard Books, 1989)

APPRECIATING DIFFERENCES

*Brown, Marcia *Stone Soup* (Scribner, 1979)

*McGovern, Ann *Stone Soup* (Scholastic, 1986)

*Ross, Tony *Stone Soup* (Puffin Books, 1990)

MORE BOOKS ABOUT SOUP

*Carle, Eric *Today Is Monday* (Philomel Books, 1993)

*Ehlert, Lois *Eating the Alphabet: Fruits and Vegetables from A to Z* (Harcourt Brace Jovanovich, 1989)

*Gerson, Mary-Joan *Why the Sky Is Far Away: A Folktale from Nigeria* (Little, Brown & Co., 1992)

*Gustafson, Scott *Alphabet Soup: A Feast of Letters* (Contemporary Books, 1990)

*Modesitt, Jeanne *Vegetable Soup* (Macmillan, 1988)

*Sachar, Louis *Monkey Soup* (Knopf, 1992)

*Rylant, Cynthia *An Angel for Solomon Singer* (Orchard Books, 1992)

Bread

BOOKS TO READ ALOUD

*Dragonwagon, Crescent *This Is the Bread I Baked for Ned* (Macmillan, 1989)

*Morris, Ann *Bread, Bread, Bread* (Morrow, 1993)

APPRECIATING DIFFERENCES

*Marshall, James *Hansel and Gretel* (Dial Books for Young Readers, 1990)

*Lesser, Rika *Hansel and Gretel* (Putnam, 1989)

MORE BOOKS ABOUT BREAD

*Czernecki, Stefan *The Sleeping Bread* (Hyperion Books for Children, 1993)

*dePaola, Tomie *Tony's Bread: An Italian Folktale* (Putnam, 1989)

*Dragonwagon, Crescent *Half a Moon and One Whole Star* (Macmillan, 1986)

*Forest, Heather *The Baker's Dozen: A Colonial American Tale* (Harcourt Brace Jovanovich, 1993)

*Lobel, Arnold *Ming Lo Moves the Mountain* (Greenwillow Books, 1982)

*Migutsch, Ali *From Grain to Bread* (Carolrhoda Books, 1981)

*Nobens, C. A. *The Happy Baker* (Carolrhoda Books, 1979)

Tea

BOOKS TO READ ALOUD

*Shaw, Nancy *Sheep Out to Eat* (Houghton Mifflin, 1992)

*De Regniers, Beatrice Schenk *May I Bring a Friend?* (Macmillan, 1989)

APPRECIATING DIFFERENCES

*Cauley, Lorinda Bryan *The Town Mouse and The Country Mouse* (Putnam, 1984)

*Wallner, John *City Mouse—Country Mouse and Two More Tales from Aesop* (Scholastic, 1987)

MORE BOOKS ABOUT TEA

*Bunting, Eve *Clancy's Coat*
(Frederick Warne & Co., 1984)

*Hutchins, Pat *The Doorbell Rang*
(Greenwillow Books, 1986)

*Mora, Pat *A Birthday Basket for Tia*
(Macmillan, 1992)

*Murphy, Jill *Five Minutes' Peace* (Putnam, 1986)

*Noble, Trinka Hakes *The King's Tea* (Dutton, 1983)

*Penner, Lucille Rech *Tea for Two...or More:
The Tea Party Book* (Random House, 1993)

*Polacco, Patricia *Thunder Cake*
(Philomel Books, 1990)

Rice

BOOKS TO READ ALOUD

*Dooley, Norah *Everybody Cooks Rice*
(Carolrhoda Books, 1991)

*Friedman, Ina R. *How My Parents Learned to
Eat* (Houghton Mifflin, 1987)

APPRECIATING DIFFERENCES

*Tompert, Ann *Bamboo Hats and a Rice Cake:
A Tale Adapted from Japanese Folklore* (Crown, 1993)

MORE BOOKS ABOUT RICE

*Ashley, Bernard *Cleversticks* (Crown, 1992)

*Delacre, Lulu *Arroz Con Leche: Popular Songs
and Rhymes from Latin America*
(Scholastic, 1989)

*Demi *In the Eyes of the Cat: Japanese Poetry
for All Seasons* (Henry Holt and Co., 1992)

*Hamanaka, Sheila *Screen of Frogs: An Old
Tale* (Orchard Books, 1993)

*Martin, Patricia Miles *The Rice Bowl Pet*
(Crowell, 1962)

*Mosel, Arlene *The Funny Little Woman*
(Dutton, 1972)

*Snyder, Dianne *The Boy of the Three-Year
Nap* (Houghton Mifflin, 1988)

Potatoes

BOOKS TO READ ALOUD

*McDonald, Megan *Potato Man*
(Orchard Books, 1991)

*Polacco, Patricia *Mrs. Katz and Tush*
(Bantam Books, 1992)

APPRECIATING DIFFERENCES

*Steptoe, John *Mufaro's Beautiful Daughters:
An African Tale* (Lothrop, Lee, & Shepard
Books, 1987)

*Huck, Charlotte S. *Princess Furball*
(Greenwillow Books, 1989)

MORE BOOKS ABOUT POTATOES

*Anno, Mitsumasa *Anno's Journey*
(Philomel, 1981)

*dePaola, Tomie *Jamie O'Rourke and the Big
Potato: An Irish Folktale* (Putnam, 1991)

*Sherman, Eileen *Odd Potato: A Chanukah
Story* (Kar-Ben Copies, 1984)

*Turner, Dorothy *Potatoes*
(Carolrhoda Books, 1989)

Pancakes

BOOKS TO READ ALOUD

*dePaola, Tomie *Pancakes for Breakfast*
(Harcourt Brace Jovanovich, 1978)

*Nordqvist, Sven *Pancake Pie*
(Morrow Junior Books, 1985)

APPRECIATING DIFFERENCES

*Galdone, Paul *The Gingerbread Boy*
(Clarion, 1983)

*Lobel, Anita *The Pancake*
(Dell, 1992)

MORE BOOKS ABOUT PANCAKES

*Carle, Eric *Pancakes, Pancakes* (Scholastic 1992)

*dePaola, Tomie *Fin M'Coul, The Giant of Knockmany Hill* (Holiday, 1981)

*Hirsh, Marilyn *Potato Pancakes All Around: A Hanukkah Tale* (Jewish Pubn. Society, 1982)

*Kasza, Keiko *The Wolf's Chicken Stew* (Putnam, 1987)

*Kellogg, Steven *Paul Bunyan: A Tall Tale* (Mulberry, 1993)

Beans

BOOKS TO READ ALOUD

*Falwell, Cathryn *Feast for 10* (Clarion Books, 1993)

*Kuklin, Susan *How My Family Lives in America* (Macmillan, 1992)

APPRECIATING DIFFERENCES

*Kuklin, Susan *How My Family Lives in America* (Macmillan, 1992)

MORE BOOKS ABOUT BEANS

*Haskins, Jim *Count Your Way through China* (Lerner Publications, 1988)

*Jordan, Helene *How a Seed Grows* (HarperCollins Children's Books, 1992)

*Kellogg, Steven *Jack and the Beanstalk* (Morrow Junior Books, 1991)

*Scieska, Jon, and Smith, Lane *The Stinky Cheese Man and Other Fairly Stupid Tales* (Viking, 1992)

Eggs

BOOKS TO READ ALOUD

*Polacco, Patricia *Rechenka's Eggs* (Philomel Books, 1988)

*Polacco, Patricia *Just Plain Fancy* (Bantam Books, 1990)

APPRECIATING DIFFERENCES

*Polacco, Patricia *Chicken Sunday* (Philomel Books, 1992)

*Polacco, Patricia *Rechenka's Eggs* (Philomel Books, 1988)

MORE BOOKS ABOUT EGGS

*Aylesworth, Jim *The Folks in the Valley: A Pennsylvania Dutch ABC* (HarperCollins Children's Books, 1986)

*Heine, Helme *The Most Wonderful Egg in the World* (Macmillan, 1987)

*Hoban, Russell *Bread and Jam for Frances* (HarperCollins Children's Books, 1986)

*Robart, Rose *The Cake That Mack Ate* (Little, Brown, & Co., 1987)

*Sans Souci, Robert D. *The Talking Eggs* (Dial Books, 1989)

*Turner, Dorothy *Eggs* (Carolrhoda Books, 1989)

Corn

BOOKS TO READ ALOUD

*Chocolate, Deborah M. Newton *Kwanzaa* (Children's Press, Inc., 1990)

*Taylor, C. J. *How Two-Feather Was Saved from Loneliness: An Abenaki Legend* (Tundra Books, 1990)

APPRECIATING DIFFERENCES

*Garza, Carmen Lomas *Family Pictures/Cuadros de familia* (Children's Book Press, 1990)

MORE BOOKS ABOUT CORN

*Aliki *Corn is Maize: The Gift of the Indians* (HarperCollins Children's Books, 1976)

*dePaola, Tomie *The Popcorn Book* (Holiday, 1978)

*Dragonwagon, Crescent *Alligator Arrives with Apples: A Potluck Alphabet Feast* (Macmillan, 1992)

*Pallotta, Jerry *Victory Garden: Alphabet Book* (Charlesbridge Pub., 1992)

*Soto, Gary *Too Many Tamales* (Putnam, 1993)

*Williams, Sherley Anne *Working Cotton* (Harcourt Brace Jovanovich, 1992)

*Young, Ed *Moon Mother: A Native American Tale* (HarperCollins Children's Books, 1993)

Nuts

BOOKS TO READ ALOUD

*Martin, Bill Jr., and Archambault, John *Chicka Chicka Boom Boom* (Simon & Schuster, 1989)

*Grifalconi, Ann *The Village of Round and Square Houses* (Little, Brown, & Co., 1986)

APPRECIATING DIFFERENCES

*Young, Ed *Lon Po Po: A Red Riding Hood Story from China* (Philomel, 1989)

*Hyman, Trina Schart *Little Red Riding Hood* (Holiday House, 1983)

MORE BOOKS ABOUT NUTS

*Benitez, Mirna *George Washington Carve:, Plant Doctor* (Raintree, 1989)

*Ehlert, Lois *Nuts to You* (Harcourt Brace Jovanovich, 1993)

*Westcott, Nadine B. *Peanut Butter and Jelly: A Play Rhyme* (Dutton, 1992)

*Wolfman, Ira *My World & Globe: An Interactive First Book of Geography* (Workman Publishing, 1991)